QUANAH
PARKER

Len Hilts

QUANAH PARKER

Gulliver Books

Harcourt Brace Jovanovich

San Diego   Austin   Orlando

HBJ

Requests for permission to make copies of any
part of the work should be mailed to:
Permissions, Harcourt Brace Jovanovich, Publishers,
Orlando, Florida 32887.

Library of Congress Cataloging-in-Publication Data
Hilts, Len.
Quanah Parker, Comanche chief.
Bibliography: p.
Summary: Traces the life of the American Indian chief
who led the Comanches in the battle for their homeland
and remained their leader on the reservation where he
guided the people in accepting their new life.
1. Parker, Quanah, 1854–1911—Juvenile literature.
2. Comanche Indians—Biography—Juvenile literature.
3. Indians of North America—Biography—Juvenile
literature. [1. Parker, Quanah, 1854–1911. 2. Comanche
Indians—Biography. 3. Indians of North America—
Biography] I. Title.
E99.C85P384   1987   973'.0497 [B] [92]   87-8488
ISBN 0-15-332879-7   (Library: 10 different titles)
ISBN 0-15-332937-8   (Single title, 4 copies)
ISBN 0-15-332997-1   (Replacement single copy)

Designed by Kate Nichols
Endpaper map by EarthSurface Graphics

Printed in the United States of America

To Ben and Colin,
who first went down Quanah's trail
with me.

Contents

About This Story . . .

This is the life story of Quanah Parker, the great Comanche war chief. It is based on historical fact and eyewitness accounts, and is as accurate as variations within the source materials permit.

It must be remembered that each event, each battle, and even each leader was seen in a different light by the Indians, the soldiers, the traders, the ranchers, and the farmers. These different viewpoints are reflected in what was remembered and written later.

Quanah, to the Comanches, was a brave, fierce, and fearless leader who fought the white intruders to protect the buffalo hunting grounds on the Staked Plains—as a matter of tribal survival.

Quanah, to the soldiers who fought him, was a brilliant adversary but a cruel, ruthless savage. Army men felt the only good Indian was a dead one. To them, the Indians were not defenders of their homes, but marauding savages to be conquered.

To the traders, Quanah and the Comanches were a source of fine horses and profit.

The farmers and ranchers believed the land they fenced belonged to them. It had been there for the taking, and they had taken it. They did not consider that it had ever belonged to the Indians. They did not see the Indian attacks on white ranches and wagon trains as defensive, but as unjustified, horrible, and barbaric actions—a source of constant fear.

This story is told for the most part from the viewpoint of Quanah and his Quohada band of Comanche Indians, whose hunting grounds were the Staked Plains of western Texas.

The Comanches, when speaking to each other, tended to speak rather formally, without contractions such as *I'm* or *can't*. In telling this story, however, we have used contractions to make reading easier.

When speaking to settlers or soldiers, the Comanches spoke a Pidgin English that slowly disappeared as they became more familiar with the English language. A typical phrase might be "Me talkum you." To avoid having them sound like comic characters, we have not used Pidgin English in any scenes.

QUANAH PARKER

Chapter

1

Comanche Boyhood—1857

Quanah sat astride Kanaki his pony and watched as Mi-so rode for the target.

Quanah felt good here, riding with his friends Mi-so and Tow-pet. He enjoyed the soft warmth of Kanaki's body against his legs. Around him, a mild south wind rippled the grass of the great plains into soft green waves. Above, a canopy of blue extended as far as his eye could see.

He sighted a distant motion on the prairie—two men riding toward him. In a moment he recognized his father, Chief Peta Nocona, and his grandfather, the great chief Pohebits Quasho. *They come to see how well we do*, he thought.

The two chiefs stopped some distance away to watch as Mi-so rode down on the boys' target—a padded ball atop a stick held at the height of a horseman.

Quanah pretended he hadn't seen the chiefs. He yelled, "Ride, Mi-so, ride! Kill the enemy rider!"

Mi-so, his bow in his hands, controlled the pony with his knees as he sped toward the target. Smoothly he pulled an arrow from his quiver, notched it in his bow, and let it fly. The arrow thunked into the stuffed ball.

Quanah shouted, "He is dead, Mi-so! You killed him!"

Mi-so waved his bow, wheeled, and again rode full tilt toward the target. Now he swung his body low along the pony's side and aimed the arrow across its neck. Again the arrow thunked into the target.

Using only his knees, Mi-so spun the pony once more. Again he dropped low along the pony's neck. The arrow narrowly missed the target and landed in the far grass.

Almost before Mi-so's arrow landed, Tow-pet raced his pony for the target. He, too, had seen the two chiefs watching.

He scored a hit on his first try. On the second pass, his arrow passed clear through the target.

"A mighty hit, Tow-pet," Quanah yelled.

On the third run, Tow-pet tried the shot from under the pony's neck. He missed.

Quanah leaned forward with his head just behind the pony's ears to whisper, "Go, Kanaki, go," and the pony shot forward.

Quanah's body moved in rhythm with the pony as they swiftly approached the target. Quanah drew his bow and shot. The arrow hit the center of the target.

"That's a coup, Quanah," called Tow-pet.

Kanaki turned sharply as they passed the target. Quanah slid down his side, one foot anchored in the pony's braided mane. His arrow flew across the pony's neck and lodged solidly beside his first shot. Kanaki wheeled without instructions as Quanah quickly notched his third arrow.

In one fluid motion, Quanah came up to a sitting position and dropped down on Kanaki's other side. His head almost touched the tall grass as they sped over the plain. Sighting the target from under the pony's neck, Quanah shot and the arrow splintered his first hit.

"You killed him, Quanah!" Mi-so screamed. "A good coup for you!"

Quanah rode up to his friends. "That's enough for today," he said. He rode toward the chiefs, and Mi-so and Tow-pet followed.

Peta Nocona and Pohebits Quasho sat quietly on their horses, enjoying the game. Pohebits Quasho, the war chief of the Noconi Comanches, was a warrior with a long record of victories. Peta Nocona, a subchief, rode at the head of a band of younger warriors.

Pohebits Quasho smiled as Quanah's last arrow hit its target. "The boy and the pony move as one. You have trained him well, Peta Nocona."

Pride swelled Peta Nocona's chest. "He is tall," he said. "That's why he makes the neck shot. The others will do better when they, too, become taller."

"He will be a great war chief," Pohebits Quasho

said. "I see it in his face when he rides. And see, the others already follow him as they come to us."

The three boys rode up.

Mi-so said, "Quanah won. All of his arrows were true."

"You also did well, Mi-so," said Pohebits Quasho. "When your legs are longer, you will make the neck shot with ease. And you, also, Tow-pet. You draw the bow fiercely. One arrow went through the target."

Tow-pet smiled. To hear praise from great warrior chiefs was sweet music. All Comanche boys longed to become warriors. They trained for it from the time they were only five summers and given their first ponies. Their eyes sparkled as they watched the warriors ride and shoot. Each dreamed of the day he could ride with them and sit in the campfire circle to tell of his brave deeds.

Quanah stopped beside Pohebits Quasho, who said, "I remember well the first time I made a true neck shot, Quanah. I was just your age, and it made me very proud."

Quanah sat straight on his pony's back. "I did it first two days ago, but then I missed some. Now I can hit the ball every time."

Pohebits Quasho's eyes sparkled. "And now you believe you are ready to be a warrior. You want to go with Peta Nocona tomorrow, don't you?"

Quanah flushed.

Pohebits Quasho laughed. "I know how you feel, for I felt the same way. It's the right way to feel, but a warrior must also know patience. Skill at riding and with the bow are only part of what he must know."

Peta Nocona said, "He learns quickly. He'll soon be ready for the buffalo hunt."

The old chief turned his horse. "We will ride back to camp together."

The two chiefs rode side by side, with the three boys behind them. Quanah sat straight on his pony and pretended they had just won a great battle. He noticed that Mi-so and Tow-pet also were straight and solemn as they rode.

The words of the two chiefs drifted back as the group slowly rode through the tall grass toward the camp.

"The buffalo herd to the north is getting smaller," Quanah heard Pohebits Quasho say. "Our Kiowa brothers say they must hunt longer to find meat. After this year, they may not have enough."

"It's the white buffalo hunters," Peta Nocona replied angrily. "They never have enough! One hunter shoots more buffalo in a moon than The People take in a year. We take only what we need, and the herd has always fed us."

"Ay, Peta Nocona," said Pohebits Quasho, "white hunters butcher the buffalo for the hides. They leave the meat to rot on the prairie."

Quanah leaned forward to hear what the great chiefs were saying. Someday he would talk like that. He ran his hand along the soft neck of his pony, and Kanaki tossed his head and nickered in answer to the caress.

Peta Nocona said, "There are many buffalo on the Staked Plains now, but that's because no white hunters have yet come to slaughter them."

"Yet?" Pohebits Quasho asked.

"They will come," Peta Nocona said. "As sure as the vulture flies to a kill, they will come. Their greed knows no bounds."

Quanah had heard the hunting ground on which they now rode was called the Staked Plains. Hovarith, the warrior who had taught him to make a spear, told him of it.

"The white man cannot find his way on this plain," Hovarith had said in disgust. "He's like a blind man who cannot read the signs. When he rides on the plain, he becomes lost. He calls this a desert with grass, and for him it is forbidden territory."

"But white men have eyes, Hovarith. Can't they see the way The People see?"

"No, Quanah, they're different. You will learn this when you become a warrior. I'll tell you why they call this land the Staked Plains.

"Many, many summers ago, before my great-grandfather was born, Spanish soldiers rode up from Mexico into the great plains. I have heard they looked for the yellow iron they prize so highly. Many starved or died of thirst when they lost their way. Then their medicine men—*padres*, they call them—showed them how to drive stakes to mark their paths. From then on, they called this land the Staked Plains."

"But," Quanah objected, "if they staked a trail, their enemies could follow it. That's foolish, to tell your enemies how to follow you."

Hovarith held up his hand. "Quanah, you are the son and grandson of great war chiefs of The People, and someday you, too, will be a great chief. You know it is foolish. I know it is foolish. But the white men don't know it. They can't read the moon and stars, or a trail in the grass. They don't know how to listen to sounds in the wind."

Quanah's attention was drawn back to the chiefs riding before him.

"This is our land," his father said. "The buffalo are our buffalo. Yet they take them as if they belonged to no one—as if we weren't here!"

Pohebits Quasho rode with his eyes straight ahead. "Peta Nocona, we've always known that as warriors we must protect our land and horses and the buffalo from those who would take them from us. We have fought the Apache, the Sioux, and the other tribes because of this." He shrugged. "The white man brings nothing new."

"The white man is a different enemy, Pohebits Quasho," Peta Nocona said. "He wastes what the Great Spirit has given us. He kills buffalo though he doesn't need them, and soon there will be no buffalo. He fences the plain so it is no longer hunting land. He scratches the dirt and plants corn. There is no longer room for the fleet antelope, the great buffalo, or even the little prairie dog."

Pohebits Quasho's eyes were sad. "It's true, Peta Nocona. When I was a boy, we rode south to hunt with the Honey Eaters band. The prairie we hunted is now fenced. The Honey Eaters themselves have been put on fenced land the white man calls a reservation. Now the Honey Eaters dig the grass and plant corn. They are no longer warriors."

As he heard these words, Quanah imagined Mi-so, Tow-pet, and himself surrounded by a fence, digging in the ground with sticks. No ponies. No swift riding across the plain. The thought made him feel sick.

He remembered, then, how Pohebits Quasho looked when he rode out at the head of a raiding party. It was a beautiful thought that made Quanah feel better. The great chief always wore his buffalo horn headdress and the magic silver shirt that protected him from arrows and bullets. The shirt sparkled in the sun.

Hovarith had told him about the magic shirt. It was very, very old. Hovarith said it came from a Spanish chief who had worn it into battle. Truly, it was great medicine that many times had saved Pohebits Quasho from death.

Now they rode off the great prairie into the deep, hidden canyon where The People were camped. Riding across the grassy plain, a horseman could not see the canyon until he stood at its very rim. No white man had ever found it. The cool, tree-lined depths had been a safe, secret campsite for the Noconi Comanches as far back as any could remember.

The long line of tepees beside the grassy banks of the stream was a pleasant sight. A narrow rock ledge, steep in places and barely wide enough for a single horse, was the only path into the canyon. Kanaki eagerly picked his way down the steepest places with surefooted ease to get to the sweet, cool water at the bottom.

The camp was peaceful and sleepy in the late afternoon sun. Ponies nibbled grass near the tepees. Children played at the edge of the water. Babies nodded and dozed in cradleboards hanging from tree branches. Warriors talked or played games in the shade of trees.

As Quanah neared the bottom, Naudah, his mother, looked up and smiled. She was scraping an antelope hide in front of their tepee. Quanah's younger brother, Pecos, was shooting a small bow and arrow with Teebo, his good friend.

The lounging warriors looked up. The girls of the camp looked, too. Everyone could see the boys riding behind the great chiefs. Quanah rode proudly, like a warrior.

Chapter

2

Quanah Finds His Medicine—1858

Sunlight streaming through the tepee opening woke Quanah. He lay under his blanket, considering what to do on such a pleasant day. Last night, his father had said that no hunting or war parties would go out today, and his mother, Naudah, had hinted that she would like an antelope for her stew pot.

That was it! He, Tow-pet, and Mi-so could hunt the fleet antelope. To bring an antelope down, you had to ride well and shoot straight from the flying pony's back. Excited by the thought, Quanah got up.

Naudah was already stirring the cooking pot, and the tepee was full of good smells.

She smiled. "Come, Quanah, eat. It will make you strong."

Quanah pulled tender strips of buffalo meat from the pot in the center of the tepee. Gray smoke lazily curled up from the fire to the smoke hole at the top. The scent of fresh grass wafted through the tepee opening to mingle with the smell of the meat. Little Pecos was playing the buffalo chip game out in front with Teebo, whose tepee was nearby. Naudah began feeding Quanah's little sister Tau-tai-yah in her cradleboard.

After he ate, Quanah walked down the line of tepees along the riverbank. He found Mi-so and Tow-pet with Ker-pet-ah and Na-ca-ten. Quanah paused. He didn't like Na-ca-ten. He was a bully, bigger than the other boys, who liked to push them and intimidate them with his loud voice. Na-ca-ten bragged a lot, but he wasn't very good with a bow, and he didn't ride as well as Quanah, Tow-pet, or Mi-so.

As Quanah approached, Na-ca-ten said, "Here's Quanah. He can go with us."

"Go where with you?" Quanah asked.

"Up the canyon to where the water falls," he said. "We can swim and catch trout. You can come, too."

Quanah's eyes blazed. "Do I need your permission, Na-ca-ten?"

"I'm the leader of this group, Quanah. If I say you can't come, you can't."

Mi-so, Tow-pet, and Ker-pet-ah felt the tension, like the air before a thunderstorm. Quanah's eyes flashed and he took an angry step toward Na-ca-ten. Then he remembered his father's words: *A war chief acts like a leader, Quanah. He never begs, argues, or fights. He leads.*

Quanah stopped, opened his clenched fists, and

said, "I am going to hunt antelope." He looked at the other boys. "Get your ponies." Then he walked away.

The three shuffled from foot to foot for a moment, then followed Quanah.

Na-ca-ten's face twisted. "You said you would swim with me."

"Hunting antelope is more fun," Mi-so answered. "Get your pony and come with us."

"Not me," Na-ca-ten sneered. "I wouldn't follow that half-breed anywhere. His mother is white!"

Quanah whirled around. A storm rose up within him, but a strong hand gripped his shoulder. He turned to look into his father's face.

"Go," Peta Nocona said. "Hunt the antelope."

"But Father, he called me—"

Peta Nocona looked into Quanah's eyes. "Are you better with the bow than he is?"

"Yes," Quanah answered.

"Can you ride better?"

Quanah nodded.

"Are the other boys following you or him?"

Quanah looked at the group, standing a little way off.

"They follow me," he said.

Peta Nocona smiled broadly. "Then why waste your time? The names he calls mean nothing."

That afternoon, Quanah brought a soft little fawn-colored antelope to his mother. "For your cooking pot," he said, holding it out to her.

"Thank you, Quanah," she said with a smile. "You're a good hunter. We shall have antelope tonight."

Quanah watched his mother skin the antelope and cut the meat for the pot. She hummed happily as she cooked, stopping only long enough to take a bit of meat, blow on it, and give it to Tau-tai-yah to chew on.

Quanah looked at his mother's beautiful blue-gray eyes, so very different from the dark eyes of The People. His eyes were like hers. He frowned. They were the eyes of white people.

He knew Naudah was not of The People. She was a white woman, who was taken captive as a girl and raised among The People by Tabbi-nocca and his wife, Chatua, of the Tenowish band.

Naudah said, "I heard about Na-ca-ten."

"No one has called me names for many summers," he said. "The others forget that my eyes are blue. Only Na-ca-ten remembers."

Naudah said, "He's jealous."

Quanah looked sadly into the fire. "White men are our enemies and I am half white." He shook his head. "I don't want to be white."

"White men are brave, too, Quanah," Naudah said softly. "You draw your bravery from both sides. Perhaps that is better than just from one side."

"Tell me the story again."

"You've heard it so often you know it better than I."

"I like to hear it."

Naudah sighed. "I was a girl of nine summers. The Tenowish raided a place called Fort Parker. They killed the men and took the women and children. Tabbi-nocca rode away with me and gave me to Chatua. I was frightened, but Chatua was kind and treated me as a daughter. Most captives are slaves and work hard around the tepee, but Chatua had no daughter and cared much for me."

"You were white," Quanah said.

"My father and mother were white, but I don't remember them. I know we lived inside the fort, and the men grew corn and wheat in the fields outside. They came inside at night."

"Did you love Tabbi-nocca and Chatua?"

"Not at first. But in time I loved them as my own parents."

"Your skin isn't white now," Quanah pointed out.

"I have lived in the prairie sun so long that my skin is like that of The People."

"Didn't you want to go back to your people?"

Naudah shook her head. "When I was fourteen summers, a white trader tried to buy me from Tabbi-nocca. I told Tabbi-nocca that I wanted to stay with Chatua."

"And Peta Nocona?"

"His hunting party came to our camp one day when I was a young woman. He was so strong and brave on his horse that it made my heart flutter. He had many coups and scalps. We exchanged glances that day, but we didn't speak. Chatua teased me and said she could see his heart fluttering, too. Three moons later he returned. He stayed for five sleeps and spent much time near our tepee. Tabbi-nocca laughed and told Chatua that Peta Nocona was one lovesick warrior.

"Then, one morning, Peta Nocona tethered a bridal offer of five horses outside our tepee. I wanted to run out, but Tabbi-nocca made me stay in the tepee until the sun was high. He said, 'It's good for him to wait. Anyway, five horses isn't enough.'

"My heart trembled when he said this. I was afraid Peta Nocona would go away.

"Chatua said, 'He's a young warrior who probably has only five horses. He will think you refuse his offer and will look for another wife.'

"Tabbi-nocca laughed. 'Did you see his face? Peta Nocona won't look for a new wife. He'll look for more horses.'

"Chatua was angry. 'He's a fine husband for Naudah. He will soon be a war chief. Everyone says that is so. You'll drive him away.'

"Tabbi-nocca went to look at the horses and came back without touching them. Late in the day, Peta Nocona's uncle Hadnetso came to our tepee. He talked long with Tabbi-nocca. Then Tabbi-nocca took the leads of the horses and handed them to Chatua. She put them in the grazing ground with our other horses.

"I trembled when Peta Nocona came to claim me. Later I found out that Hadnetso had promised that Peta Nocona would give Tabbi-nocca five more horses the next summer.

"We left the Tenowish and went to live in Peta Nocona's tepee with the Noconi." She counted on her fingers. "That was thirteen summers past. You were born the next year as the flowers bloomed near the lake they call Laguna Sabinas."

"Did The People hate you because you were white?" Quanah asked.

Naudah shrugged. "A few did, but they forgot—

---

especially after Peta Nocona became my husband."

Quanah scowled. "I become angry when Na-ca-ten teases me. My skin is the same as his. I am the son of a Noconi chief. I am not white. It is only my eyes. None of The People have eyes like ours."

Naudah gently touched his face. "Quanah, the color of your eyes is not important. When you become a great warrior, everything else will be forgotten."

After the evening meal that night, Peta Nocona said, "I spoke to Pay-to-sun today."

Quanah caught his breath. Pay-to-sun was the medicine man. When it was time for a boy to seek his medicine, Pay-to-sun helped him. Quanah knew what lay ahead. He would find his medicine for spiritual strength, then become a buffalo hunter, and then a warrior. It would all happen by the time he was sixteen summers.

The next morning, Peta Nocona took Quanah to Pay-to-sun's tepee. Pay-to-sun's brown face was wrinkled like old leather, but his voice was kind as he invited Quanah to sit beside him outside the tepee.

"Quanah and I will talk," he told Peta Nocona, who left them alone. Pay-to-sun said, "It is time to put aside the games of boys. You must seek your medicine."

Quanah sat very still to hide his mounting excitement. He had waited many summers for this moment.

"You are the son and grandson of great warriors," Pay-to-sun said. "A warrior needs courage and strength. He must have strong medicine to guide his arrows straight, give him wisdom in battle, and lead him to the best hunting grounds."

Quanah and his friends had often talked about the medicine of the warriors. Everyone knew when a warrior had strong medicine because it showed in his deeds. Each warrior wore a medicine bag around his neck with the tokens of his medicine in it, and he never went into battle without it.

"To find your medicine is not easy, Quanah. You must fast and pray to the Great Spirit. You must make a journey and wait for a vision. No one knows what signs you will see. You may pray many times before the Great Spirit allows you to know your medicine, but it will come when the time is right."

As he spoke, Pay-to-sun brought out his pipe and put tobacco in it. "I will pray now that you receive your vision," he said. He lighted the pipe, blew the smoke toward heaven, then chanted in a low voice, "Great Spirit, hear me as this smoke carries my words to you. Look upon this boy, Quanah, and grant him the vision that will tell him of his medicine."

Quanah listened to the old man's deep chant. Inside, he felt different already. His boy thoughts were fading, and in their place he felt a serious longing.

"When must I seek my medicine, Pay-to-sun? And where must I go to do this?"

"After Peta Nocona came to me yesterday," Pay-to-sun said, "I prayed to the Great Spirit. Now I know that before the sun disappears tomorrow, you must go to your medicine place. Until then, speak to no one. Spend your time in deep thought. Begin your fast

---

17

today and do not eat the evening meal. Tomorrow, bathe in the stream to purify yourself. Then, late in the day, walk alone up the path from the canyon with only your bow, your pipe, and your buffalo blanket. Go to the hill with the trees that is toward the place where the sun hides each night. You know the place?"

Quanah nodded. The hill, crowned by a grove of trees, stood like a sentinel in the midst of the prairie.

"Smoke and pray four times on your journey to the hill. Once there, sleep so you face the place where the sun is reborn. Greet the new sun each morning and ask that the vision be granted. Pray all day and watch for signs. Many things will happen, but when the true sign comes, you will know it.

"Stay in your medicine place for four sleeps. If no sign comes, return to the camp."

Quanah walked from Pay-to-sun's tepee up the canyon and sat on a ledge to think about what he must do. Like all The People, he felt the presence of the Great Spirit all around, a part of everything they did. As he looked down on the tepees below, he felt he could see the Great Spirit hovering over the camp.

The sun was high. "Great Spirit," he said, "I seek a sign from you. I pray you to show me the way."

Quanah bathed in the stream, then put on his breech-clout. He took his bow, his pipe, and his blanket and started up to the rim of the canyon, keeping his eyes straight ahead and looking at no one. At the top he prayed, then walked out across the flat prairie toward the hill. The sun was dropping in the sky.

He paused twice more in the prairie to pray and reached the hill just as the sun dropped from sight. In the twilight, he climbed to the top of the hill and spread his blanket on the ground. He watched the light fade and heard the night noises begin. Hunger pulled at his stomach. Stars filled the sky, and he chanted a prayer Naudah had taught him. He lay rolled in his buffalo skin, facing the point where the sun would rise in the morning.

Sleep would not come. Quanah felt frightened, hungry, and alone. Animals moved in the trees around him, and their eyes blazed like fire coals in the night. His heart was heavy. What if he had no vision? What if his medicine did not come?

He awoke just as the bright edge of the sun peeked over the rim of the earth. Facing the growing red ball, he chanted, "O Great Spirit, I am Quanah and I seek my medicine. Show me the sign."

Throughout the day he prayed and chanted. Sometimes he faced the sun. At other times he lay facedown on the ground with his arms extended. He saw deer and coyotes and a wolf nearby, watching him. Hawks wheeled in the sky. There was death somewhere out on the prairie, for vultures circled like black shadows. By evening, he could barely stand his hunger and thirst.

On the second day a herd of antelope crossed the prairie below, pausing often to graze. The sun heated the hilltop, and perspiration trickled down Quanah's chest. Late in the afternoon a plume of smoke rose in the sky to the south. As darkness settled in, the air cooled.

Quanah again rolled himself in his buffalo skin. He slept fitfully, dreaming strange dreams and waking between them. On the third morning his legs trembled as he rose to face the sun. His mouth was dry, and his belly cried for food.

He watched the sky, the prairie, even the animals for a sign, but saw only life on the prairie as always. He chanted his prayers, but heard no answer. He saw a spider spin a long, thin web in a bush, a sign that the weather would be dry. Spiders spun thick, short webs only before rain. In the distance a huge herd of buffalo moved across the plain. On a bush near his medicine place, plums grew a ripe purple, and as he gazed at them, his hunger grew.

During that night the sound of a black bear thrashing somewhere down the hill woke him. He had seen a swarm of bees during the day and knew that the bear was after their honey. The thought of the honey made Quanah's mouth water.

On the fourth day, when the sun was at its highest point, Quanah became dizzy and light-headed. He slept between prayers, and his sleep was full of wild dreams. When he lighted his pipe to send his prayers to heaven, he became dizzier and fell to the ground. He struggled to continue his praying and chanting.

Late in the afternoon he saw a great bald eagle circling overhead. Suddenly the eagle swooped toward him. As the bird approached the earth, it snatched a snake from the ground a few feet from where Quanah stood. Grasping the helpless snake in its talons, the eagle soared skyward. A feather from its wing wafted down and settled at Quanah's feet.

Groggy and confused, Quanah picked up the feather. At the same time he seemed to hear a voice chanting a song. He listened carefully, for this was the medicine song he would sing for the rest of his life:

> *I am the eagle, strong and fast,*
> *I fly far and take what I need,*
> *My eye is clear, my courage great,*
> *No enemy can vanquish me.*

The voice whispered that he must keep his medicine strong. He must never eat when anyone stood behind him, and he must never eat the flesh of a bird. The eagle and the snake, the voice said, are in your future life in ways you cannot know.

A great happiness flooded him. He laughed out loud and, in spite of his weakness, felt good. He had had his vision, for the eagle was his medicine and it was strong. The snake was an ancient sign of The People. The Great Spirit had given him his song and the taboos that always accompanied strong medicine.

Quanah fell to his knees and gathered the two pebbles between which the snake had been. He put these, along with the eagle's feather, in a pouch that would be his medicine bag. Later he would add the claw of an eagle. Then he thanked the Great Spirit for his vision.

Walking down the hill wasn't difficult, but pushing through the deep grass of the prairie required all his energy. He came down the path into camp just as the sun set.

Pay-to-sun was waiting as Quanah stumbled from

the path. "I have had a vision," he said. "The eagle is my medicine."

Pay-to-sun held up his hand. "Tell no one of the vision, Quanah. They may know that the eagle is your medicine, but that is all." He slipped his arm around the boy to support him as they walked to Peta Nocona's lodge.

"Tomorrow," he said, "you must build your own tepee beside that of your father. Keep your medicine in your own tepee. Eat with Peta Nocona and Naudah if you like, but sleep always in your own tepee."

Peta Nocona and Naudah met him with food in front of the tepee. "Sit and eat," Peta Nocona said, with pride in his voice.

"Eat slowly," cautioned Naudah. "Your belly has been empty for too long."

That night Quanah slept on the ground near Peta Nocona's tepee, once again rolled in his buffalo skin. Before he slept, he felt a deep satisfaction. He had strong medicine.

Chapter

3

Quanah Kills His
First Buffalo—1858

Quanah rode Kanaki up the hill near the new camp and looked out across the prairie. A great buffalo herd covered the grassy plain like a moving blanket.

"Aiyee!" Quanah cried and pressed his knees into Kanaki's side. He rushed to tell Peta Nocona they had found the great herd. The Noconi had moved camp three times during the past moon, tracking the buffalo.

As Quanah rode into camp, he found the women still putting up tepee poles, unpacking the mules, and starting cooking fires. The chief stood outside his tepee.

"Peta Nocona!" Quanah shouted. "The buffalo are here!" Breathless, he jumped from Kanaki's back. "There are more buffalo than blades of grass on the prairie."

Peta laughed. "Good, Quanah. Tomorrow we hunt."

Then he became solemn. "Are you ready to join the hunt?"

Quanah had waited long to hear those words. He danced and waved his arms in joy, then suddenly remembered he was now a hunter. He looked sheepishly at Peta Nocona.

The chief smiled broadly and said, "It's good to celebrate, my son."

The chief called Marsenti, the camp crier. "Tell The People we will hunt tomorrow," he said.

Marsenti walked through the camp, crying the news in a strong voice.

Peta Nocona turned back to Quanah. "You know you must follow the directions of the hunt leader?"

"I know," Quanah said. "I have watched many hunts."

"Listen carefully, Quanah. I am the hunt leader. We will surround the herd in a great half-moon, forcing them to come together. At the right moment I will signal, and the hunters will ride in for the kill."

Quanah said, "I know what to do."

Peta Nocona eyed him. "Not so fast, my son. I know you are eager, but a hunt is even more dangerous than battle. If someone makes a mistake, the buffalo stampede, and many hunters are hurt. If you are the cause, you will not be welcome around the fire tomorrow night."

"I will ride in only when you give the signal," Quanah said. "I have practiced—"

Peta Nocona gently placed his hand on Quanah's shoulder. "This is your first hunt. Killing the buffalo is dangerous work even for experienced hunters. You will ride near the edge of the herd as the hunters go in."

Quanah lost his smile.

Peta Nocona said, "It is important. If any buffalo break away, you must turn them back into the herd. If you do not, the strays could surround the hunters, and that, too, is dangerous."

He looked hard at his son. "You will do nothing foolish? You will do as I say?"

Deflated, Quanah said, "Yes, Father," and went slowly to his own tepee. He had dreamed so often of riding into the buffalo herd! He had watched the great hunters. It was hard to imagine himself riding at the edge and not in the thick of the hunt. He brooded for a while, then said to himself, *Hey, at least I'm joining the hunt*. His spirits rose a little.

The next morning the hunters quietly formed a wide half circle behind the huge, slow-moving herd. From his position behind the hunters, Quanah could see the main herd stretching endlessly before him, its dust blurring the sun.

The hunters worked their horses slowly along both sides of the herd, forming a kind of pincers. Gradually they pressed their ponies inward, massing the buffalo together.

Other young hunters rode near Quanah. Behind them, the younger boys and women led pack mules that would carry the buffalo hides and meat back to camp after the hunt.

Suddenly Peta Nocona gave a piercing cry and threw

up his right arm. The other hunters yelled and turned their horses sharply toward the buffalo. The pincers closed in on the moving herd. Frightened by the yelling hunters, the buffalo bellowed and began to gallop.

Skillfully keeping their ponies behind the sharp horns and tossing heads of the buffalo, the hunters each chose a shaggy target and rode within spear range. By now the big beasts were wild-eyed, making perilous work for the hunters. One misstep could throw hunter and horse under the pounding hooves or into the slashing horns.

Quanah was guiding Kanaki to the right of the herd when the pony stumbled and nearly fell. He recovered quickly but Quanah suddenly remembered the prairie dog holes in the grass. Kanaki's foot must have caught in one. To show he was all right, Kanaki spurted forward. Quanah patted his neck.

Quanah's heart pounded as he rode in the noise, heat, and dust. The big animals jostled one another, and Kanaki, alert and quivering, galloped closer to the herd. Sweat glistened on his coat.

Quanah had watched many hunts. He had felt the earth tremble as buffalo herds stampeded, but riding close like this was different. He felt icicles of fear. If the herd swerved suddenly or if some of the animals broke loose, the moving mass could swing in front of him. Kanaki was only half the size of a buffalo and would be crushed between their huge shoulders.

Without warning, a huge leader bull, his head as big as a boulder, swerved from the herd. Quanah watched other buffalo turn to follow him. If they escaped from the body of the herd, they would overrun and trap the hunters in front of them.

Quanah slapped Kanaki's flank. The pony leaped forward and galloped to the side of the big bull. Quanah shouted, "Turn him, Kanaki! Turn him!"

As the pony and the buffalo ran side by side, Quanah steered Kanaki against the buffalo. Quanah could feel the hot, shaggy hide against his leg. Slowly Kanaki edged the big beast back toward the herd. Resisting, the buffalo swung his head to snag Kanaki with his horns, but the little horse danced nimbly away.

Quanah looked back. A dozen other black forms loomed in the dust cloud behind him, forming a small, dangerous herd of their own. Their eyes blazing with fright, they headed for the open prairie. Quanah knew that turning the big bull back now wouldn't stop the strays. The leader had to be killed.

He swung his spear to his shoulder. Kanaki veered to the right, moving away from the buffalo to allow Quanah room for the throw. The big bull trumpeted. His horns, a spear's length from Quanah's leg, cut the air like slashing knives.

Abruptly Kanaki swerved toward the buffalo, and Quanah drove the spear with all his strength into the buffalo's side just behind his heart. The buffalo bellowed in pain, stumbled, then crashed to the ground. The force of his fall wrenched the spear from Quanah's hand. Kanaki almost went down, but jumped to one side just in time.

Quanah wheeled Kanaki and turned to the buffalo behind him. The other young braves had moved up, and Quanah joined them. Together they forced the stray buffalo back toward the herd.

Peta Nocona signaled the hunters to withdraw, and the hunt was over. They had killed as many buffalo as The People could carry. The clan would have meat and robes for months. The remainder of the herd rumbled on across the prairie. Quanah and Kanaki rode back to where the women and children were now preparing the fallen buffalo.

Naudah, with her sharp knife, was expertly stripping the hide from the big animal Quanah had speared. Other women cut steaks and strips of meat to put in bags on the pack mules.

"You killed this bull like an old hunter," she said as he rode up. "It was a very brave deed."

Quanah slipped from Kanaki's back to look at the buffalo's head. It was the biggest he had ever seen, truly the head of a great buffalo chief.

"He has fine horns," Quanah said.

"I thought you would end up on them," Naudah replied. "I saw how close you came."

For a moment Quanah relived the fear he had felt near the pounding herd. Then he said, "I would like those horns. They will make a fine headdress."

Naudah nodded. "You shall have them."

In camp the women put some of the meat to dry in the sun to make jerky. Naudah took several hides for a new tepee cover. After the skin was cured, she would scrape the hair from it and make paintings of the great deeds of her husband Peta Nocona.

That night the crier called The People to the center of the camp. Around the blazing fire they feasted on fresh buffalo and had a victory dance. Each hunter came forth to tell of his own brave deeds during the hunt: how many buffalo he had slain, and how close to the herd he rode to drive his spear into a buffalo's heart. The People cheered as each told his story.

Finally Peta Nocona said, "We have a new hunter tonight."

As the people quieted, he called Quanah forward. Quanah walked proudly to the fireside. The flickering light danced on his cheekbones and across the muscles of his chest.

A woman sitting next to Naudah said, "He is handsome."

Naudah whispered, "He looks much like Peta Nocona."

"You should be proud," the woman replied.

Quanah told how the big bull buffalo broke away from the herd. He said he knew the bull had to be killed because only that would stop the other buffalo from running over the hunters. They would turn only if their leader went down.

"I drove my spear into his heart on the first try, and when he fell, the others became frightened. We pushed them back into the herd before they could surround our hunters."

The People cheered. Peta Nocona said, "My son, from now on you will ride with our hunting parties. In your honor, according to our custom, I give gifts."

He motioned to Naudah, who brought out great

slabs of buffalo meat. Peta Nocona gave these to older clan members who no longer hunted. He gave three ponies to young warriors who had but few ponies of their own.

Quanah went to his tepee that night happier than he had ever been. He was a hunter who had killed his first buffalo.

Chapter
4

The Texas Rangers—1858

Visitors came to the camp of Pohebits Quasho. Among them were the war chiefs of other Comanche bands— the Penatethkas or Honey Eaters, from the south; the Quohadas or Wanderers, from the Staked Plains; and the Kotsotethkas or Buffalo Eaters. They gathered to celebrate the success of the spring hunt, and the chiefs talked around the fire.

Now that Quanah was a hunter, he too sat with the chiefs and listened.

White Bear of the Quohadas spoke of the wagon trains moving west through Kansas. "Five summers ago," he said, "the white chief said the plains would be ours if we no longer attacked their farms or took their horses. But they lied. The wagons now cross our plains at many places."

Eagle Claws of the Buffalo Eaters agreed. "We see

the soldiers and the wagons. We see how they fence the land. Their promises are broken. We must stop them."

Toshaway of the Honey Eaters asked, "Haven't we had enough fighting? We lose many brave young warriors each summer. Now more soldiers come with guns that outreach our arrows."

The other chiefs murmured among themselves. One said accusingly to Toshaway, "You took the Honey Eaters to the white man's reservation."

Toshaway answered with great dignity, "They offered us land and seed. We accepted. Now our children will have fathers, and our women will have husbands. There is no more killing. We live in peace."

White Bear stormed around the fire. "That is the talk of cowards. The white men make you slaves and pen you in like tame animals."

Toshaway turned a sad face to the group. "I prayed in the sacred places," he said, "and listened to the Great Spirit. I hear what you say, but it came to me that if we continued to fight, we would all die. The Honey Eaters do not want to die."

Pohebits Quasho looked at Toshaway. "I am sorry for you. You live among the Texans, our worst enemies. How can you believe their promise that life on the reservation will be good? The Texans want all of us dead. You will be the first."

Toshaway said, "What will you do when there are ten times as many white men? Think hard upon this. We do what we must."

Then Toshaway and the Honey Eaters left the camp to return to the reservation in Texas.

Pohebits Quasho told the chiefs, "We do not agree with the Honey Eaters. We believe it is better to die than to be penned. For two summers the white men have closed in. To stop them we made many raids and took many horses, but still they come like ants from an anthill.

"The only way to stop them is to attack every farm, burn every wagon. We must make them fear us. Only then will this land be ours."

The chiefs around the fire murmured agreement. Quanah listened to Pohebits Quasho and also agreed.

"Look at this list, Rip!" Hardin Runnels, the newly elected governor of Texas, said as he pointed to the paper on his desk. "A hundred ranches attacked, ranchers killed, mutilated, their women carried off! And it's getting worse."

"Nothin' new about that, Governor," Colonel John Ford replied. "The Comanches been killing Texans since 1836."

Ford, square jawed and leathery faced, was the Texas Rangers' most experienced officer. He was known as "Old Rip" because he signed his casualty reports with the letters R.I.P., which stood for "Rest In Peace."

Runnels slammed his fist on the desk. "We're going to stop it and stop it now!"

"Don't expect the Army to do it, Governor. They don't know much about fighting Indians. They ride out in columns, so any Comanche worth his salt knows they're comin' half a day ahead."

Runnels sighed and dropped into the chair behind his desk. "Rip, you're an Indian fighter. How would you do it?"

"Simple, Governor," he said. "Fight Indians in Indian fashion. Don't march whole regiments at them. Sneak up and raid like they do. Track 'em to their camps and hit 'em when they aren't lookin'. That's what we did in the old Texas Rangers." He tamped tobacco into his pipe and grinned. "But you didn't invite me here just to find out how to fight Indians, Governor."

"No," Runnels said. "We need you, Rip. The Legislature has money to equip a force of a hundred men, Ranger style. I want you to head it up and go after the Comanches. Clean them out of Texas."

"Why me, Governor?"

"You know Indians and Indian fighting, Rip. You know most of the old Rangers, the good frontier fighters. Get them. Appoint your own officers. Make your own plans. Just get the Comanches out of Texas."

Ford puffed thoughtfully on his pipe. "I'm a mite old for this kind of thing, Governor—but you've got your man. I want a hundred Indian scouts along with the Rangers. And I want Sul Ross to run them."

"You mean old Captain S. P. Ross's son? He's only twenty, Rip."

"He grew up fighting Indians alongside his daddy, Governor. He knows 'em."

"All right, Rip. It's your war. But are you sure you want Indians with you?"

"I want Tonkawas, Governor, from the Brazos Reservation. They hate Comanches more than Texans do; they'd travel a month to get a shot at one. We can have them scout ahead and smell out the Comanches. Then we'll fight them Indian fashion, not like the Army."

Runnels stuck out his hand. "How soon can you be ready to go?"

"A couple of weeks," Ford said, "if I quit jawing with you and get to work."

Ford made his base camp on the Brazos River. His Rangers were seasoned frontiersmen, tough and clear-eyed. Their uniforms were the rough buckskins and wide-brimmed hats of the frontier. They rode their own prairie-trained horses and carried their own trusty guns.

Sul Ross recruited the Tonkawa scouts on the reservation, then joined Ford. As the two men looked over the force, Ford said, "Don't look much like soldiers, do they, Sul?"

Ross grinned. His face was young, but his eyes were old and experienced. "Good thing, else I wouldn't be here."

That night Ford, Ross, and Chief Placido of the Tonkawas devised a plan. The Tonkawas were to range out across the prairie and find the Comanches. The Rangers would attack any bands they found.

A week later the scouts reported there were no Comanches in Texas, but many were north in Indian Territory.

"That's out of your area, Rip," Sul Ross said, "not in your jurisdiction."

Ford grinned. "If they are there this month, they'll be here next month. Anyway, what do I know about geography? My job is to find Indians. The governor's orders say to follow all hostile Indians and inflict punishment on them."

"Then let's get to riding," Ross said.

With the scouts fanned out in front, Ford's Rangers broke camp on April 22, riding each day from dawn to dusk. They followed the rivers—the Brazos, then the Red. They skirted the Wichita Mountains and headed for the Canadian River. By May 10, they were on the Oklahoma plains with Indian signs all around them.

Ford dismounted. "This bunch just finished hunting," he said. "The drag marks are deep. They're pulling travois loaded with buffalo meat. I'd say they're headed for camp to butcher and smoke the meat."

The Tonkawas discovered the Comanche camp in the Antelope Hills, a string of low, sandy mountains near the Texas/Oklahoma line. These hills had long been a secret Noconi fortress—a place to hide after raids in Texas and Mexico. It had always been safe from white soldiers.

The Rangers rested near the hills while the scouts probed ahead. The Tonks returned with the news that the Noconi were there, along with the Buffalo Eaters and the Tenowish. Old Iron Shirt himself, Pohebits Quasho, was the head chief, and second to him was Peta Nocona, chief of the Noconi. Pohebits Quasho had the front camp, with Peta Nocona camped several miles farther back.

Ford called his fighters together. "They haven't seen us yet," he said, "so now we travel fast. There'll be no campfires, no noise. We'll slide on our bellies if we have to. I want to hit them while they're in their lodges."

Swiftly the group mounted and rode out.

That night they made a cold camp and rolled up in their blankets for a quick sleep. The stars were still bright when they swung back into their saddles. The silent column came on the first Comanche tepees just as rosy streaks spread across the eastern sky—six lodges near the river edge. There was no movement in the Comanche camp.

Ford squinted at the lodges. "This is just a watch camp. We'll have to take it quickly so they can't warn the main body."

The Tonkawas swooped down on the camp, whooping their war cries. They slashed at the lodges with their spears, and then fired as the awakened Comanche braves rushed out to meet the attack. Within five minutes the lodges were leveled and all their occupants dead.

At that moment a lone warrior who hadn't heard the battle rode from behind a hill. When he saw the devastation, he turned his horse and fled toward the river, crossing at a shallow point just above the camp.

Ford yelled, "He's going to warn the main camp!"

The Rangers charged after the warrior, splashing across the slippery river bottom, but by the time they reached the other side, he had disappeared. The Rangers followed his tracks.

They raced around a small rise and suddenly came

into full view of the big Comanche camp just as the sun topped the verdant hills. The lodges stood like pointed sentinels in an arroyo that led up from the clear waters of the Canadian.

Three hundred Comanche warriors hastily formed a line across the arroyo between their women and the advancing Rangers. Still smearing war paint on their bodies and faces—black, for war and death—they raced into position. Topped by bison-horn headdresses, they brandished their spears and shrieked war cries.

Ford hesitated. He was in for a pitched battle he hadn't planned on. The Rangers, battle-tried veterans, waited, looked at the Indians, and calmly checked their rifles.

Following an old Indian custom, Comanche warriors rode one at a time into the field between the two forces. As each galloped down the hill, he shook his spear at the Tonkawas, challenging them to individual combat.

Several Tonkawas started out, but Chief Placido called them back. Angrily, the braves returned. They wanted to fight.

Finally a great Comanche chief, resplendent in war gear, rode out. The newly risen sun glinted on his silver armor.

"Well, look at that!" Ross said to Ford. "Old Iron Shirt in his Spanish armor! The Indians claim his shirt is such strong medicine that you can't kill him when he wears it."

Pohebits Quasho pranced proudly back and forth, shaking his spear and calling his challenge.

"He looks like one of those knights of old," Ford said.

A Tonkawa marksman took careful aim with his rifle and fired. The bullet went true, and Pohebits Quasho threw his arms skyward as he fell from his horse.

A howl rose from the Comanches. Pohebits Quasho had fallen! Warriors rode out to raise their great chief, but Tonkawa bullets drove them back. All eyes were on the fallen body. Pohebits Quasho's medicine had failed! The sacred iron shirt had not saved him from death.

Seizing the moment, Ford ordered the Tonkawas to attack. "Draw them to the left," he told Chief Placido. "We'll charge from the side as they run at you."

Placido signaled with his spear, and, howling shrilly, the Tonkawas followed him while the Rangers held their position. Eager to fight, the Comanches charged the racing Tonkawas.

As the two forces met, Ford yelled, "Charge!" and the Rangers stormed the exposed Comanche flank.

Pandemonium erupted. The shouts of the Rangers mixed with the triumphant Tonkawa cries and the war whoops of the fighting Comanches. The wailing of the Comanche women floated above the din.

When the Rangers hit their flank, the battle quickly turned against the Comanches. The Indians fell back, fighting desperately and giving ground slowly in a running battle. They ducked into timber groves and behind rocks to make a stand and then move on, holding each position as long as possible to give their families time to escape.

For three hours, the fight slowly moved up the arroyo. Then the Rangers wearied and returned to the Comanche campsite.

They found five hundred Comanches, with Peta Nocona at their head, waiting for them.

Seeing the new threat, Ford rose in his stirrups and yelled, "Hit 'em now!"

With revolvers blazing, the Rangers and Tonkawas charged the Comanches. In the first run, twenty warriors went down. Then the Indians launched a counterattack, assuming that after the first volley, the Rangers would be defenseless while they reloaded their guns.

The Comanche counterattack was usually deadly, but this time the warriors rode straight into a hail of bullets. The Rangers hadn't stopped to reload but had kept on shooting. For the first time, the Comanches faced six-shooters, a gun new to the West.

More warriors fell. The failure of the counterattack and the continuous firing confused the Indians. Their battle line broke, and they retreated up the arroyo.

Quanah and the young braves sat on their ponies at the edge of their camp. Earlier they had heard the sound of a battle, and Peta Nocona had ordered his warriors to mount. Before leading them to the battle, he had commanded the young braves to stay and protect the women and children. Now they listened anxiously as the battle sounds came closer.

As the screaming and gunfire grew louder, Quanah

knew that the battle was moving up the arroyo toward them.

Suddenly the warriors came into view, and he saw that they were retreating. The hard-riding Rangers charged them time after time. Though they were outnumbered three to one, the Rangers and Tonkawas kept pushing the desperate Comanches back, not giving them time to establish battle positions.

Quanah caught a glimpse of his father running from rock to rock, shouting orders and trying to rally his warriors. But the Rangers attacked again and again. Quanah desperately wanted to ride out to help the warriors, and Kanaki danced impatiently under him, anxious to see action. But Quanah held back, for they had an important job to do.

As the warriors retreated toward the camp, Quanah saw that the battle had turned completely against them. It was time for him to move.

He turned Kanaki and yelled to Naudah and the other women, "Quick! Follow me."

He led the women up the narrowing arroyo, away from the battle and into a dense thicket.

"Stay behind me," he shouted, pushing the branches aside. He knew these hills well, for he hunted in them every summer. Beyond the thicket was a small hidden path that led up the side of the arroyo. He waited while all the women, carrying their small children, started up the path. Then he and Kanaki closed in behind.

Following faint trails, the group fled north through the mountains. They spent the night cold and hungry in a small clearing. Mi-so and Tow-pet, who had escaped with them, went back along the trail in the morning and reported that the Rangers had left for their own camp.

Young hunters went out after game in the nearby hills. The women made fires and cooked what the hunters brought in. After everyone had eaten, they talked about what to do.

Quanah said, "We will go to the campsite two sleeps beyond the mountains and wait for Peta Nocona."

The others agreed, and they set out for the new campsite.

It was four days before all The People were reunited. Peta Nocona was one of the last to come in.

The Comanches counted their dead and mourned them. Peta Nocona and the other chiefs stood at the campfire and swore vengeance.

"We will kill ten for each warrior who died," Peta Nocona said. "It will be a bloody summer."

All Texas hailed Rip Ford's victory. This would stop the Indian raids! Ford's Rangers were disbanded.

But within weeks, raiding started again along the frontier. All that summer the Comanche bands rode hard, and the revenge they took was violent. No rancher, no wagon train, no rider was safe from their savage attack.

The violent outburst shocked the Texans. Once again they demanded action against the marauders.

Chapter
5

The Battle of Wichita Mountains—1858

General Twiggs of the U.S. Army ordered Major Earl Van Dorn and his Second Cavalry against the Comanches. Over the summer Van Dorn built Camp Radziminski, a stockade in the heart of Indian country. When he was ready, Sul Ross and the Tonkawa warriors joined him.

Working from the new outpost, the Tonkawa scouts found a large camp of Comanches ninety miles away in the Wichita Mountains. Remembering the lessons learned from Rip Ford at Antelope Hills, the Second Cavalry pushed the ninety miles in thirty-seven hours, staying in the saddle sixteen hours at the end without a break. On October first, they moved into position for a dawn attack on the Comanche camp.

The camp was quiet in the crisp autumn air. Feeling secure in their hideout, the Comanches slept. Five hundred horses grazed in the mist near the edge of the village as Sul Ross and the Tonkawas crept up to drive them from the remuda.

The lodges were strung out along the banks of a stream. At sunrise Van Dorn charged the upper end of the village, while Sul Ross led a second unit against the lower end.

Startled Comanche braves rushed from their tepees to find their horses gone, and desperately fought the mounted troopers on foot. Gunsmoke mingled with the morning fog to cover the battle with a dense pall.

Later a trooper said it was like fighting ghosts in a graveyard.

In the smoky fog Ross chased shadows running for the river—only to discover they were women and children fleeing. He ordered an Indian scout to take one little white girl prisoner. Suddenly Comanche warriors emerged from the mist, and Ross found himself surrounded. Two cavalrymen with him were shot from their horses.

Ross swung his Sharp's rifle to his shoulder, but before he could get off a shot, a warrior grabbed a downed cavalryman's gun and fired. Ross felt the bite of the bullet and with horror, recognized his assailant as Mowhee, a Comanche he had known as a friend at his father's frontier post. Mowhee drew his knife and leaped toward him.

Over the din of battle, a Comanche voice shouted an order and Mowhee turned. A cavalry officer fired, and Ross watched Mowhee pitch forward, dead. At the same moment, a Comanche arrow ripped Van Dorn's flesh. Then the remaining warriors faded into the smoke and mist.

The troopers counted ninety dead Comanche warriors. The People had also lost all their horses, equipment, and supplies.

"They'll have a tough winter," Ross told Major Van Dorn the next day as the two lay in a hospital tent. "There's not much hunting time left."

Only five cavalrymen were killed. The troopers buried their dead, then built litters pulled by mules to carry the wounded men back to the stockade.

Ross's Indian scout brought the little white prisoner to him. She was about twelve years old and spoke no English. Ross talked to her in Comanche and learned she had been taken captive about ten years before. She didn't remember her name or her parents. She insisted she was "one of The People."

As his wound mended, Ross talked often to the little girl and they became friends. Unable to find her family, Ross adopted her and she grew up as his daughter, Lizzie.

At the first sound of the attack, Quanah had thrown back his buffalo robe and run from the lodge. Discovering that Kanaki was gone, he tore back to the lodges, where he found Naudah and Pecos. He quickly led them away from the fight. Naudah cradled little Tautai-yah in her arms as they ran through the fog.

Around them, the warriors fought savagely to allow the women and children to get away. Quanah and Naudah made their way between the lodges to the edge of the camp, avoiding the fights that were taking place. Finally they struck off across the prairie, away from the village. Hidden by the mist, other families joined them.

That night the band that came together made camp with very little, since their food and lodges had been destroyed. Quanah and Naudah waited anxiously by a tiny fire, and as each group of weary defenders straggled in, they ran to see if Peta Nocona was among them.

Each day Naudah's fear grew. Finally, after three days, Peta Nocona brought in the last of the warriors. There were no scalps, no victory songs—only wounds, mourning, and defeat.

Peta Nocona said little. He was now the war chief of the northern Comanche bands, who must lead The People to a safe place and replenish their food.

Late one night he sat with Quanah near the fire. Naudah, Pecos, and the baby slept under a single buffalo robe near them.

Quanah, too, was silent and thoughtful. The two battles of this summer were his first taste of real defeat. As a boy he had looked forward to the return of the jubilant warriors, driving their captured horses and displaying their prisoners. He loved the victory celebrations.

Tonight, sitting with his father, Quanah thought about defeat and death, and, for the first time, he realized the burden a chief of The People must carry.

"The white men fight in a different way now, Quanah," Peta Nocona said. "Twice this summer they have come seeking battle, when they never attacked before."

Quanah said, "Father, our camps have been safe in these mountains. Why were we not safe this summer?"

Peta Nocona spat into the fire. "The Tonkawas joined the white man and led him to us. But there is still a place where no white man dares to go: the Staked Plains. The white man will not follow the Tonkawas to the great plains. There our camps will be safe."

He thought for a long time, then said, "The white soldiers now have pistols that shoot many times as they ride. One soldier can kill many warriors. We cannot face them as we have in the past."

"Pohebits Quasho gave us wise words," Quanah replied. "He said if we make them fear us, they will go away. When we strike suddenly to raid their ranches and burn their wagons, they fear us. Small raids are good. Then there is no big battle where we lose many warriors to their guns."

Peta Nocona was surprised at his son's wisdom. He smiled. "Quanah, you have learned well, and what you say is true. We'll move our lodges to the great plains. From there, we can fight in small raiding parties. Then The People will be strong again."

Quanah said, "We need horses, father. There are horses on the ranches and at the forts."

"You think we should raid now for new horses?"

Quanah nodded. "The soldiers think we are beaten and they are not afraid. We must make them fear again."

◆   ◆   ◆

Peta Nocona led his people to Palo Duro canyon.

Quanah loved this beautiful canyon, especially when the cottonwoods turned golden yellow amongst the dark green junipers and framed the towers of bright red rock that rose from the canyon floor. A sweet fork of the Red River flowed gently along the floor of the canyon.

Quanah showed Pecos the wonders of Palo Duro. As the air turned sharp in late autumn, he taught him to make bows and arrows from the hard wood of the juniper. He led him up the steep path to where the hard flint for arrowheads, knives, and scrapers could be found.

"Pecos," he told him, "we are safe here. Only this path leads to our camp, and it's so narrow and slippery that riders must come down in a single file. We can kill anyone before he reaches the bottom."

"Do the soldiers know of this place?" Pecos asked.

"No," said Quanah. "They are afraid to ride in the plain. But even if they did, they couldn't find our canyon."

As winter set in, the Buffalo Eaters, returning from raids in Mexico, visited the Noconi. They came with bad news about the Honey Eaters.

Skin-of-a-Bear, the war chief, said, "On the reservation, the white man gave them seed to grow corn and a good man to teach them, Robert Neighbors." Neighbors, he said, taught the Honey Eaters to plant seed, and their farms prospered. The Honey Eaters saw that the new way of life might truly be better than the old.

"But then white settlers saw that their crops grew well and wanted the land," Skin-of-a-Bear went on. "As the fields grew green, the Texas soldiers told the Honey Eaters they must move to another reservation. The white man had lied again.

"The Honey Eaters were given only a day's notice to move. They asked to stay long enough to harvest their crop, so they would have food for the winter. But the Texans said no. They led the Honey Eaters to a new reservation on dusty land east of the Wichita Mountains. The white men promised them food for the winter, but none came."

Wolf's Tail, another warrior, said, "The good man Neighbors fought the greedy men who wanted the rich reservation land, but no one listened to him. The Honey Eaters were moved and their crops were left to rot. Then the white men killed Robert Neighbors."

The People listened with sadness. Peta Nocona said bitterly, "It is always the same. The white man has proved again that he cannot be trusted."

As he went to sleep that night, Quanah tasted hatred. The feeling was to last for many years.

Chapter
6

Naudah Is Taken Captive—1860

The People shivered through the winter, fishing and hunting to stay alive. In early spring they hunted buffalo, drying the meat to replenish their food supply and using the skins to build new lodges. Between hunts, Comanche raiders roared down the trails of the frontier, stealing horses. By late spring the herd was rebuilt and The People were eager to settle their score with the Texans.

Quanah was now fourteen summers and taller than the other young hunters. His arms and chest had thickened, and his body was well muscled. As the winter softened into spring, he ached to revenge the loss of his beloved Kanaki and the bitter defeats of the past year.

One day while hunting deer, Quanah spied a horse in a ranch-house corral. Like Kanaki, this horse had fire in his eye and held his head proudly. His broad shoulders and deep chest hinted at endurance, and he moved well around the corral.

Quanah hid in the grass until the moon rose, then crept toward the corral. Suddenly the deep bark of a big dog broke the silence. Quanah waited silently on his belly. In a moment the ranch-house door opened and yellow lantern light spilled into the night. Two men came out carrying rifles. They walked around the house and the corral, looking carefully. One passed ten feet away and Quanah's hand went to his knife, but the rancher walked on.

"Old Rufe's nervous tonight," he said.

"It's the full moon," the other replied. "That always makes him skitterish."

The men went back into the house and closed the door.

Quanah opened the corral gate and jumped to the back of the horse he wanted. With a wild shout, he galloped through the gate, driving four more horses ahead of him.

The ranch door flew open, and the crack of rifle fire cut through the night air. Quanah dug his heels into the horse's side. The ranchers fired a dozen times, but couldn't take aim in the tricky moonlight. In a few minutes Quanah was out of range.

The horse felt good under him as they galloped across the prairie. He had a long stride and responded quickly to knee pressure. Quanah knew he had selected well; this horse would make a fine hunter.

He leaned forward. "I will call you Chotah," he said softly. "We will hunt and fight together."

◆　　　◆　　　◆

Comanches swept the frontier all summer, raiding ranches, scalping settlers, taking horses, and driving off stock. Nearly every rancher saddled up to ride out against them. The intensity of the fighting increased until the frontier blazed in a full-scale war. Daily reports of burned-out ranches whipped the Texans to a frenzy, and Peta Nocona's name struck terror in every settlement.

Sam Houston, the new governor of Texas, called on the Army for help. Colonel M.D. Johnson marched a regiment into the plains, but failed to kill a single Indian. Peta Nocona's raiders followed the troops and taunted them by stampeding their horses at night. The soldiers returned to the fort on foot, sore and embarrassed.

That autumn Peta Nocona made a bloody raid through Jack and Palo Pinto Counties, well east of the frontier, then struck the flourishing communities above Waco.

In desperation Governor Houston called on Sul Ross. "We need action, Sul," he told him.

Ross rounded up forty tough old Rangers and twenty soldiers of the Second Cavalry, telling them they had only one objective: hunt down the raiding Comanches.

In the full moon of early autumn, Peta Nocona led his band back to their old camp on the Pease River. Towering cliffs of red, yellow, and blue clay sheltered the camp in the winter. Mesquite wood for the campfires and dry grass for the horses were plentiful.

At the camp, Peta Nocona called the subchiefs to his lodge. He smoked his pipe, offering the first puff to the sun, the second to the earth, then puffs to the four winds. Then he passed the pipe around the circle.

The chiefs wanted more raids on the white settlements. "We have not yet avenged our dead," said Buffalo Foot.

Peta Nocona shook his head. "As I hunted this morning, a wolf jumped up. He looked at me, then howled three times. Another wolf across the hills to the east answered. Wolves do not often howl in the daytime. Esa, the wolf, is the brother of The People. He was warning us not to go east, where the white man is."

After hearing Peta Nocona, the others agreed. The wolf medicine was very strong, and the four howls were important. This was indeed a sign.

"We'll hunt buffalo one more day," the chief said, "for winter food. Then we'll listen to brother wolf and go to the canyon on the plain. Tomorrow, as the women break camp, we hunt. Then we move."

Two hunting parties went out. Peta Nocona led one; Quanah joined the other. The buffalo herd covered miles of prairie, and each party attacked a separate flank.

After the hunters left, Naudah began to pack the family's belongings. With her Mexican slave, José, she piled blankets and cookware in big baskets. José attached the cedar poles of the travois to the packhorses and as each basket was filled, lashed it to the poles.

Ross knew the hit-and-run tactics of the Comanches well. To beat them, he used the old Ranger ploy— trail the Indian to his lair and strike without warning.

Seventy cowboy volunteers joined the Rangers and had tracked the Comanches to the Pease River by early December.

Bitter "blue northers" were already shooting cold waves into Texas. Riding hard, the Rangers braved the weather huddled in sheepskin coats.

At first the Rangers failed to find the well-hidden Comanche camp, though there were plenty of signs of the Indians. Then Ross saw vultures circling in the sky ahead of them, and the troopers spotted the front-runners of a large herd of buffalo coming from the north.

"Must be Indians hunting at the back of that herd," Ross said. "Vultures are always there for the butchering."

Ross and two Rangers scouted up an arroyo. Ross looked over the crest and saw a hundred Comanche lodges in a valley not two hundred yards away. Located on the banks of a little stream, the camp was well protected by high cliffs.

The Comanches were breaking camp. Some lodges were already down, and women were strapping baskets on the travois of pack mules. Ross hurried back to his Rangers and ordered a charge.

Naudah ran from the lodge at the sound of gunfire, only to see shouting Rangers and bluecoats charging through the unprepared camp. Those warriors remaining in camp were overwhelmed before they could get their weapons. Within moments the lodges were flattened and their defenders killed. Man-of-Long-Hair burst from his lodge next to Naudah's, carrying his spear, and fell instantly with blood spurting from a bullet wound in his chest.

Discovering that they were surrounded, the rest of the disorganized Comanches fled in every direction.

Naudah grabbed Tau-tai-yah and leaped to her horse's back. "José!" she cried. "Mount! Ride!"

Mimsonah, daughter of Man-of-Long-Hair, wailed over her father's body in front of their lodge.

"Pick her up," Naudah ordered José, who leaned down to grab Mimsonah as he rode past. She rode behind him on the horse.

Pecos was not near the lodge. Naudah called his name but before he could answer, she saw two riders galloping toward her with guns drawn.

She kicked her horse's side. She and José sped through the tepees and away from the camp. Naudah glanced back. Two men, one in a blue uniform, rode hard after them, yelling for them to stop.

Both Naudah and José urged their horses on. The soldier pulled up alongside of Naudah. He aimed his gun at her, and she quickly reined her horse. She held out the baby to him. White men, she knew, seldom killed babies.

The lieutenant was surprised. "A woman!" he said. "I thought you were a warrior."

Sul Ross, the other rider, kept after José. He fired, and Mimsonah fell like a broken doll from José's horse. José fell, but bounced to his feet with his bow ready to shoot. He let fly an arrow that grazed the white man's shoulder.

Ross shot again and shattered José's left arm. With

his arm useless and his bow broken, José ran to a tree and turned to face the soldier. He saw death coming and began to chant a death song he had learned from Peta Nocona.

Ross walked toward him, covering him with his pistol. "Surrender!" he said in Comanche. "Kneel down!"

José snarled and lunged at him. Ross shot him dead.

"Wonder who he was," Ross said, looking at the body. "He fought like a chief."

A soldier nearby was talking in broken Spanish to some women prisoners being brought in. Most of The People knew Spanish through their trade with the Comancheros from Mexico.

One said, "He is Nocona's. Nocona's José."

The soldier had difficulty understanding her. After she repeated it several times, he recognized the chief's name.

"Captain," he shouted. "She says this is Nocona. You got the chief himself. No wonder he fought the way he did."

Later in his report, Ross paid tribute to Peta Nocona's brave fight and counted him as one of the battle casualties. Peta Nocona, however, was several miles away, hunting buffalo.

The lieutenant brought Naudah to Ross. "Just a squaw!" he said. "They all dress and ride the same. What a waste!"

Ross looked at Naudah's blue eyes. "Wait a minute, lieutenant! Look at her blue eyes! This is a white woman."

Naudah stood straight and silent, holding her baby as the officers discussed her in excited tones. More prisoners were brought in. Naudah saw that neither Peta Nocona nor her sons were among them.

"We'll take 'em all back to the fort," Ross said.

Chapter

7

Peta Nocona Dies—1861

When Peta Nocona returned to the camp, he found only death and devastation. An eerie silence hung beneath the cliffs. Nothing moved in the wreckage of the lodges.

Quanah came back to find Peta Nocona examining their slashed tepee covering. Quanah went to him.

"They have taken Naudah," the chief said in a flat voice.

"And Tau-tai-yah?" Quanah asked.

As Peta Nocona nodded, the small figure of Pecos burst from the woods. With tears streaming down his face, he flew to Peta Nocona and threw his arms around his legs.

"The soldiers came," Pecos wailed. "They took mother. I ran into the woods."

Peta Nocona picked Pecos up and held him until

the sobs subsided. He said to Quanah, "We must leave now and take our dead with us. We will mourn later."

Deep gloom covered the camp through the winter. The People cut cedars to make new lodge poles. Quanah slept in the lodge with Pecos and Peta Nocona, but each one remained wrapped in his own private thoughts.

One evening, Quanah broke the silence. "Will you take another wife, father?" he asked.

Peta Nocona slowly shook his head. In a low voice, he said, "There is no other Naudah. None can replace her."

The Comancheros came to the Staked Plains from Mexico each year to barter with The People. A warrior with many horses to trade could get guns, tobacco, and cloth—whatever he wanted—when the Comancheros came looking for fine Comanche horses.

Quanah always enjoyed the excitement of the Comanchero trading camps. The traders stayed for several weeks, while the Kiowa, Arapaho, Cheyenne, and even the Sioux came to barter. Between the trading, the braves played games and raced, and there was much talk. Quanah met old friends, made new ones, and heard news of the other Comanche bands.

The Noconi had few horses to trade this year, but Juan, with whom Peta Nocona often traded, said, "Chief, take what you want. I'll be back before the snow flies. Give me horses then."

Juan gossiped as Peta Nocona looked over the trading goods. "We met the Mescalero Apache as we came north," he said. "They raided settlements in Texas and had many horses."

"The Apache!" Peta Nocona said. "Why are they on our hunting ground?"

Juan shrugged. "The hunting is better than in Arizona and New Mexico."

"They don't belong here," Peta Nocona told the chiefs later. "We must drive them off."

After the Comancheros returned to Mexico, Peta Nocona led The People toward Apache country. The warmth of spring had touched the plains and sprinkled colorful flowers through the grass. The soft scents of April brightened Quanah's spirits, though an empty feeling remained in him. He missed Naudah sorely.

Peta Nocona rode in front of the long line of horses and travois as the band traveled. The sun and the sweetness of the air lifted The People's gloom, and they laughed again. The children played when they camped. At the thought of the coming battle, the warriors sat straighter on their horses.

The Apache were old enemies. They had intruded on Comanche hunting grounds before and had to be driven off. Now they were back again to be dealt with.

In the mountains of red rock in New Mexico, Peta Nocona chose a campsite, and The People put up their lodges. Quanah watched his father lead the warriors out in search of the Apache. Quanah was not yet a warrior, and only warriors went to battle.

When the warriors had been gone for nine sleeps, Pecos asked, "Why are they gone so long?"

"Riding in the mountains is slow, Pecos," Quanah told his little brother. "And they must find the Apache camp. They'll be back soon."

On the eighth day Quanah and Tow-pet hunted for small game along a trail leading into craggy mountain passes. As they paused at a stream to drink and rest their horses, Quanah found a young eagle lying dead on a rock. He spotted the eagle's nest on a ledge high above.

"It fell from its nest," he told Tow-pet. "It wasn't ready to fly."

Chotah whinnied and shied away from the dead bird. Quanah stroked the horse's neck and walked him along the path away from the clearing. Then the boys mounted and rode back to the camp.

Finding the dead eaglet disturbed Quanah. The eagle was his medicine. He went to see Pay-to-sun, and they smoked a pipe together in front of the old man's lodge.

"It is a sign of evil, Quanah. Bad medicine."

On the tenth day the war party returned. The battle with the Apache had been long and fierce. Four of Peta Nocona's warriors were slain, but the Apache lost many more and had fled.

"They will not ride our lands again," Hovarith assured Quanah. "They have learned."

The war party carried Peta Nocona back. In the fight, an Apache spear had opened a huge hole in his side, and he was in great pain. The warriors laid him in his lodge. Quanah sent Pecos to seek the healer.

Quanah sat next to his father and bathed the wound with clear water.

Peta Nocona said, "I feel the closeness of the Great Spirit. I think it is time to die."

Quanah looked at his father's strong features. Now the furrows, which had always given his face strength, were deeper, and his bronze skin pale. Beads of perspiration stood out on his forehead. *He is in pain,* Quanah thought. *He looks very old and tired.*

"Quanah," Peta Nocona said, "call the chiefs to me."

The healer applied herbs to the wound to relieve the chief's pain. Quanah brought the subchiefs of The People. They sat in a circle, facing Peta Nocona.

Peta Nocona said to them, "Go back to the Palo Duro canyon. But do not stop the raids. Keep the white man full of fear. That is your only hope."

Bends-the-Back said, "We stay here until you can lead us, Peta Nocona."

The chief shook his head and softly sang his death chant. His voice was weak, but the chant filled the quiet lodge. Quanah listened and tears touched his cheeks. Then the voice faded and the lodge was silent. Everyone watched Peta Nocona's face.

Suddenly he cried, "O Great Spirit!" in a loud voice. His eyes closed and his head turned to one side.

"He is gone," Bends-the-Back said.

Quanah and Pecos were orphans. Peta Nocona was dead and Naudah a captive. According to the customs of The People, to insure that his spirit did not return to haunt the band, Peta Nocona's sons had to leave the camp and live with other Comanche bands. To show their grief, Quanah and Pecos had to give away all their possessions.

Pay-to-sun came to the lodge. "I will send Pecos to Eye-of-the-Owl of the Yampareka band," he said. "He is a friend and will raise him well."

Quanah nodded. He felt great sadness at being parted from his little brother, but he knew that they both must accept the law. He gave Peta Nocona's horses to other families, keeping only Chotah for himself.

"Where will you go?" Pay-to-sun asked.

"Does it matter?"

"You are full grown," Pay-to-sun said. "You are tall and straight with the body of a warrior and the skill of a hunter."

"But I am not yet a warrior," Quanah said. "I have no wealth, nothing but Chotah."

Pay-to-sun pointed to the medicine bag around Quanah's neck. "You have the strong medicine of the eagle, Quanah. Do not forget it. This is a time of testing—as a warrior is tested in battle. Call on your medicine for strength."

Quanah embraced Pecos and gave him to Pay-to-sun.

"Good-bye, little brother," he said, with tears in his eyes. "Grow strong." Then with his bow and his spear, he mounted Chotah. Without looking back, he rode toward the Staked Plains.

Quanah rode to the camp of the Buffalo Eaters, to the lodge of Esa-bivi, the chief. He told him of Peta Nocona's death and asked permission to live with the clan.

Esa-bivi said, "Your father was my friend. You may put your lodge at the edge of our camp, but remember you are no longer a chief's son. Now you will tend our horses."

"I am a hunter," Quanah said.

"You may hunt with us, but not as a chief's son."

Quanah's new life in the Buffalo band was lonely. He had no friends and no wealth. With the Noconi, he had been a chief's son who would one day be a chief. Among the Buffalo Eaters, he was only a boy who cared for the horses.

He was never allowed to lead. On one hunt, he spied a bear in some trees near the hunters.

"A bear," he called out, "over here." But the other hunters kept riding along the trail.

So Quanah stayed by his own tepee and kept watch over Esa-bivi's many horses. After each buffalo hunt, they gave him a small portion of the meat. *I live*, he thought bitterly, *on the tribe's charity.*

More than a year passed before Esa-bivi called Quanah to his lodge. The Buffalo Eaters had crossed the border into Mexico and raided two villages for Mexican mules. Now they prepared to raid a third.

"We need warriors," Esa-bivi said. "You are old enough and have a fine body. Tomorrow you ride with the warriors."

That night Quanah hefted his spear and tried his bow. He remembered that he was the grandson of Pohebits Quasho and the son of Peta Nocona. Though he would ride behind the main body of raiders the next day, he felt good.

The raiders charged into the sleepy Mexican village as the villagers took their siesta. Those who awoke and resisted were killed. Near the center of town a troop of Mexican soldiers attacked the Indians from behind the buildings. A fierce fight developed.

Quanah rode into the battle with his spear ready. A soldier crouching behind a wooden bench aimed his long rifle at Esa-bivi, who did not see him. Quanah urged Chotah forward and speared the soldier before he could pull the trigger.

The battle was short. The soldiers retreated quickly when they realized they were outnumbered. Esa-bivi and his warriors rode triumphantly back to camp with their captives and mules.

Later in the Buffalo camp, as the warriors sat in a half circle around a buffalo hide spread on the ground, victory dancers chanted and pranced to the beat of drums. Then each warrior rode into the circle, thrust his spear into the buffalo hide, and told of his deeds.

Esa-bivi stood up and said, "Quanah saved my life today."

Quanah rode into the circle and drove his spear into the buffalo hide. He said, "I am Quanah."

Everyone listened as he told of killing the Mexican soldier who was about to shoot Esa-bivi. Those who had seen it said, "What he says is true."

"Come down and join the company of warriors, Quanah," Esa-bivi said. "You are no longer a boy, but a man!"

During the next year, Quanah rode on many raids with the Buffalo Eaters and collected many coups. He earned the respect of the other young warriors. He was no longer lonely, but he still felt distant from them—an outsider.

As the trees began to lose their leaves, the Quohada band—The Wanderers—came to visit. The Quohadas lived deep in the Staked Plains. Yellow Bear, the Quohada war chief, had known Peta Nocona well. He sat by the fire with Quanah the second night of the visit.

"You like the Buffalo band?" Yellow Bear asked.

Quanah shrugged. "They are good people. They fight well."

"But you are not happy with them?"

Quanah did not reply. Yellow Bear looked at him shrewdly. He saw a taller-than-average, strongly built, handsome warrior, who, though still young, had clear eyes and the look of courage. As he neared manhood, Quanah had come to look more like his father. Yellow Bear saw that, too.

"Ride with the Quohadas, Quanah," Yellow Bear said. "We would like you to be one of us."

Chapter

8

Quanah Marries Weckeah—1866

Quanah joined the Quohadas as a warrior and quickly found friends among the other young warriors. Fiercest of the Comanche clans, the Quohadas respected Quanah for his ability as a fighter, and he soon became a leader. When he proposed a hunt or a raid, many followed him.

His memories of the bad years after the loss of his mother and the death of Peta Nocona slowly faded. He longed to see Pecos again, and his heart leaped in joy one day when his hunting party came upon the Yampareka camp. He hurried to the lodge of Eye-of-the-Owl, who was mending a bow in front of the lodge.

When Quanah asked for Pecos, the older warrior shook his head sadly.

"He died three moons ago, Quanah," he said. "It

was a bad fever. We did what we could, but it wasn't enough. The Great Spirit took him."

Quanah walked away, his feeling of joy displaced by one of great sadness. First his mother, then his father, and now his little brother. The feeling of deep loneliness returned and was with him for many moons.

Among Quanah's new friends was Weckeah, the daughter of Yellow Bear. Quanah liked to talk with her. They laughed together and picked berries. She loved colorful flowers, and Quanah brought her many. When he hunted deer and antelope, he brought them to her as gifts. She mended his moccasins and sewed beads on his shirt. She was like a sister to him.

One day Quanah looked at Weckeah, and she no longer seemed like a sister. Suddenly he stuttered when he talked to her and became clumsy in her presence. Weckeah, too, changed. Before, she had walked freely into his tepee. Now she became shy and came to his tepee no more.

On long rides Quanah had always concentrated on what might lie ahead. Now he was distracted. He thought always of Weckeah. On long nights away from the camp, he looked at the moon and wished she were beside him.

One day the warriors returned from a raid just at dusk. Quanah left his weapon in his own lodge and went to the lodge of Yellow Bear to see Weckeah. As he approached, he heard the sound of music.

Tannap, the son of Eckitoap, sat outside Yellow Bear's lodge, playing Comanche love songs on a reed flute. He played and sang for a long time. Quanah, hidden behind a tepee, watched and was angry. His anger surprised him, for there was no reason why Tannap should not play and sing if he wanted to.

Weckeah did not come out. But Tannap's message was plain to Weckeah, Yellow Bear, Quanah, and the whole camp. Tannap courted Weckeah and wanted to marry her.

Quanah was furious. After Tannap left, he called Weckeah out. They walked together beside the stream.

"Do you want to marry him?" Quanah demanded.

Weckeah cast her eyes down. "No, Quanah." They walked awhile, then she said, "I love only you, Quanah."

"Then send him away," Quanah said.

"You know I cannot do that. I cannot choose whom I marry. My father will do that."

Quanah said, "Tannap's father, Eckitoap, has many horses. I have only a few."

Tannap serenaded Weckeah at twilight for the next two nights. He sang in a good voice, and his songs were pretty, but Quanah hated the sound.

On the fourth day, Quanah went on a raid. When he returned, Weckeah came to him, weeping. "Oh, Quanah," she said. "Tannap's father has made a bridal offer of ten ponies."

"I have only four," Quanah said.

"He will bring them tomorrow. Ten ponies are such a good price, I'm sure my father will accept. In three days Tannap will claim me and take me to his lodge."

Quanah hurried to his friends. "Lend me a dozen ponies," he asked. "I will repay you as soon as I can steal them from the ranchers."

His friends agreed to bring the ponies the following day.

Eckitoap heard of the plan. The next morning he visited Yellow Bear. "I have decided to raise the bridal offer to twenty ponies," he said.

Yellow Bear, who did not know the plan of the young warriors, was astounded. He had not expected ten ponies for Weckeah. Now Eckitoap had doubled even that price. Yellow Bear couldn't believe his good fortune. He told Eckitoap that Tannap could claim Weckeah in three days.

When Weckeah told Quanah, his face fell. "All my friends together do not have twenty horses," he said. "We are young."

Weckeah was miserable. "I do not want to go to Tannap's lodge," she said.

As Quanah talked with his friends about the problem, he had an idea. "I know how Weckeah can be mine," he said. "We will elope."

"Yellow Bear will hunt you down like a deer," Buffalo Horns said. "You will cheat him of his daughter and twenty ponies. When Yellow Bear brings her back, Weckeah will be disgraced."

Quanah's jaw hardened. "He will not bring her back. He won't find us. We'll leave the Quohadas forever."

They talked for a time, trying to decide where Quanah and Weckeah could hide to escape Yellow Bear's wrath.

Buffalo Horns said, "I could lead you to a place I know—" He stopped, thought a minute, then said, "Quanah, I will go with you."

70

Twisted Tail said, "We could all go with you."

All the young warriors agreed to accompany Quanah and Weckeah. They would leave the Quohadas and form a new Comanche band.

"We are good warriors," Buffalo Horns pointed out. "We can raid, and there are not so many to divide the horses among when the raids are over."

"You can be chief, Quanah," Twisted Tail said.

Buffalo Horns' sister carried the message to Weckeah. She whispered it into Weckeah's ear so no one would hear, but Weckeah's cry of delight almost gave it all away. Her father looked at her suspiciously, then shrugged without asking what made her so happy. After all, in two sleeps she would go to Tannap's lodge. Why shouldn't she be happy?

Weckeah crept silently from Yellow Bear's lodge and met Quanah just after the moon went down. She discovered that twenty of Quanah's friends would accompany them. Quanah told her they were all leaving the Quohadas forever. They had formed a new band, and he was to be its chief.

The group moved stealthily away from the camp, then rode all night. They did not stop until sunrise to graze the horses and eat. At noon, they split into pairs and rode again. Each pair traveled in a different direction.

"Yellow Bear will have ten trails to follow," Quanah said. "He won't know which way to go."

The band reunited a few days later near the headwaters of the Concho River, a long way from Yellow Bear and the Quohadas. They set up camp and began to raid. During the next months under Quanah, they raided throughout western Texas and built a large herd of stolen horses.

Other young warriors joined them. A few who had come with Quanah became lonesome and rode away. Many returned with wives—and new recruits. In less than a year, the band numbered a hundred warriors and had a large herd of horses for trade with the Comancheros.

Yellow Bear and the Quohadas searched furiously for Quanah and Weckeah for two moons, but could not find them. In the months that followed, travelers visiting the Quohadas brought stories of the new Comanche band, and Quanah's name became well known. But whenever Yellow Bear hurried to where the band had camped, they had already moved on. His anger smoldered like an old campfire. Quanah had cheated him and stolen his daughter.

Then he heard that Quanah and his band were trading with certain Comancheros. Yellow Bear, Eckitoap, and the Quohadas put on war paint and rode to the Comanchero camp.

Quanah's scouts saw them coming. When Yellow Bear and Eckitoap topped the hill near the Comanchero camp, they found a hundred warriors drawn up in war formation waiting for them. The two war parties faced each other on the prairie, each waiting for the other to make the first move.

Other tribes who were trading with the Comancheros watched from a nearby hill. Seeing several hundred Comanches in a fierce battle was more entertaining than races or games. They began to bet on who would win.

The spectators clapped and yelled for the action to begin, but neither band really wanted to fight. Brothers and cousins and sons faced one another, reluctant to cross the battle line.

Finally, old Running Deer, with his bent back and gnarled hands, rode out between the two groups. As the oldest chief of the Quohadas, Running Deer was greatly respected for his wisdom. He held up his hand, and in a wavering voice called Quanah, Yellow Bear, and Eckitoap to counsel with him.

The three rode out.

The old man said, "If you fight, we lose many brave warriors. We should not kill each other. We have many enemies more deserving of our spears and arrows."

The three nodded. Yellow Bear said, "Quanah has stolen my daughter."

"I know what happened," said Running Deer. "I have thought about it. Plainly, Weckeah is already Quanah's wife. That cannot be changed. It is also plain that Yellow Bear did not receive the twenty horses for his daughter."

Eckitoap said, "What about my son? His bride was stolen."

"Agreed," Running Deer said. "Now consider this. The young men who follow Quanah are all brave Quohadas. They are the lifeblood of our band. Without them, we are old warriors with no future."

The three began to speak at once, but Running Deer silenced them.

"Hear me," he said. "I say that Quanah should pay Yellow Bear twenty ponies. That is fair. I also say that he should pay Tannap nineteen ponies as damages for stealing his bride. That, too, is fair. I also say that Quanah must lead his young men back to their homes."

He looked at each of them. "Can you agree to these terms?"

"My son has lost a wife," Eckitoap said.

"She was not his wife," Running Deer said. "He can find another. The nineteen ponies Quanah gives in damages will more than pay for a new wife."

"I don't have that many horses," Quanah said. "I can give Eckitoap nineteen horses now, but can Yellow Bear wait? I know where twenty horses are penned on a ranch near here."

Yellow Bear laughed in spite of his anger. "Quanah, I like your spirit. I want you as the father of my grandchildren even without the twenty horses."

"Good," Quanah said. "Then I'll get—"

"Wait," Yellow Bear interrupted. "I'll take the twenty horses, anyway."

Running Deer cried, "Done!" and they all shook hands. The waiting warriors saw there would be no fight and broke their battle lines.

Yellow Bear cried to them in a loud voice, "Ride to Quanah's camp. There will be a feast tonight. We celebrate."

He glanced at Quanah. "You will provide the feast?"

Quanah said, "Why me?"

Running Deer, laughing, cried, "Done!" and rode away.

Quanah rode close to Yellow Bear. "We will feast two days," he said. "Tomorrow *you* pay."

The watchers, grumbling at the loss of a good show, went back to their trading.

Chapter

9

The Treaty of
Medicine Lodge—1867

During the four years of the Civil War, the Army withdrew from the frontier. With no force to stop them, the Indians raided at will, killing frontier settlers or forcing them to abandon their ranches and move to safer land.

By 1867, the government was under great pressure to restore order to the frontier. Congress established a Peace Commission, which invited all the tribes to join in a council on October 19, 1867, on Medicine Lodge Creek in Kansas. The council site, in a lovely green valley timbered with elms and cottonwoods, was far from white settlements.

Six Peace Commissioners—a senator, the Commissioner of Indian Affairs, four generals—traveled to the council site, accompanied by nine newspaper reporters.

♦   ♦   ♦

During the summer of 1867, Quanah fell very ill. High fever raged through his body. He lay in his lodge many days, too weak to speak and often delirious. Weckeah nursed him, bathing his head in cool stream water. The healer visited the lodge many times with potions and chants to drive the evil spirits from Quanah's body.

By summer's end Quanah was on his feet, but too feeble to hunt or raid.

One morning a wounded boy returned to the camp to report that during the night the band's horses had been stolen from the common grazing ground.

"Six of us were watching the horses when we were attacked," he said. "I'm the only one alive. After a warrior attacked me, I pretended to be dead."

"How many horses did they take?" Quanah asked.

"Most of them."

"Was it white soldiers?"

"No," the boy replied. "They were Indians who spoke a tongue I do not know."

Most of the Quohada warriors were away on a raid. Quanah sent three trackers to trail the horses across the plain. Although they rode hard, the horse stealers stayed ahead of the trackers, who came back after a week.

"It was a big war party," one said. "We did not dare get close. They were Navajos from the red lands of Arizona."

When the Quohada raiders returned, Bear's Ear and the other chiefs agreed to take to the warpath. The Navajos must be punished for daring to steal The People's horses.

As the meeting closed, a rider came into camp with a message. The Great Father in Washington wanted a big council of all the tribes. The Quohadas were invited to come, talk, and receive gifts.

Bear's Ear, the war chief, sneered. "They'll sing the same song as before," he said. "They'll give us gifts and demand we go to a reservation. We have more important business: the Navajos. I listen to no more empty promises."

Quanah said, "I'm too weak to fight, but I can travel. I will go to the council to hear what is said."

Quanah arrived at Medicine Lodge the day before the soldiers. He set up his tepee with the Honey Eaters who came from the reservation.

Chief Toshaway, now old and fatter than ever, greeted him. "Ah, Quanah, it pleases me to see you."

Quanah embraced him. "I hope the sun shines on you at Fort Cobb," he said.

Toshaway shrugged. "We live, Quanah. That is all. This world is not my world. I shall be glad to leave it soon."

Suddenly he called out, "Mac! Here is Quanah. You wanted to meet him."

Quanah had heard of Mac—a white man named Philip McCusker who had lived among the Honey Eaters for many years and was married to a Comanche woman.

Mac invited Quanah to smoke a pipe with him. "I knew your mother," he said.

Naudah!

"Does she still live?" Quanah asked.

McCusker shook his head. Naudah, he said, had died three years earlier—of a broken heart, some said, longing for her people. He told Quanah of her capture and the four years she spent with her white family.

"You know, she was called Cynthia Ann Parker before she was carried off by the Comanches," Mac said. "Everyone along the frontier knew about the raid on Fort Parker, and the Texans had been looking for little Cynthia Ann for years. Sul Ross, when he saw her blue eyes, knew that Naudah was white, and after he spoke with her, guessed that she was Cynthia Ann.

"To make sure, he sent for Isaac Parker, Cynthia Ann's uncle. When Parker met Naudah, he didn't think she looked much like Cynthia Ann but thought it could be her. People change in twenty-four years. Not only that, Naudah remembered the fort and the dates seemed right.

"Then, as your mother listened to the men talk, she heard them say 'Cynthia Ann' and remembered her old name.

" 'Cynthia,' she said. 'Me Cynthia.'

"Isaac Parker choked up over finding his niece and took her home to live with his family. Naudah cried and begged to go back to her own people. Old Isaac Parker couldn't figure out why she wanted to go back to the Comanches. His wife understood, though."

Quanah listened with rapt attention, remembering Naudah in the tepee, smiling and happy. The memory renewed his love for her.

Mac relighted his pipe. "Isaac's wife told him that

Cynthia didn't remember her own childhood—just life with her husband and children. She said it was no wonder Naudah wanted to go back.

"But Isaac wasn't convinced. He kept Naudah, and she learned to eat white man's food and live in a house instead of a lodge. But she never stopped grieving for Peta Nocona, Pecos, and you, Quanah.

"She lived with the Parkers for about four years, growing more and more sad each day. She ate little and cried every day. Then little Tau-tai-yah caught a bad fever. Naudah nursed her and they even got a white doctor, but Tau-tai-yah died."

Quanah thought of happy little Tau-tai-yah in her cradleboard. He couldn't believe she was dead.

"After that Naudah just gave up. A little while later, she died, too."

"Cynthia Ann Parker." Quanah rolled the name on his tongue.

Mac nodded. "Among white men, because you are her son, you would be Quanah Parker."

Quanah smiled. "I want to honor the memory of my mother. Now I will be Quanah Parker."

The Peace Commission, accompanied by Army units in full dress, made a ceremonial entry into the council site. Bands blared a march, and flags flew. Impressively, they paraded over a hill and down to the river, where an open shelter had been built. Two hundred troopers of the Seventh Cavalry, with the sun glinting on their rifles, flanked the closed wagons in which the members of the Peace Commission and the reporters rode. Stretched out behind the wagons for two miles, like the long tail of a kite, were hundreds of white-canvassed freight wagons, pulled by six-mule teams. The wagons carried gifts for the chiefs.

The troops came to parade rest, and the commission members took their places at tables in the shelter. At that instant an ear-shattering war whoop echoed throughout the valley. Thousands of Indians suddenly appeared in a mass on the crest of the hill, galloping at full speed in tight formation. They rode in a huge "V," its point toward the soldiers. Then they smoothly formed five moving circles, one within the other, and became a giant multicolored wheel of riders whirling on the prairie.

The five wheels then closed into one massed circle five layers deep. The circle moved toward the gathered commissioners and opened to create a wide lane leading to the meeting tables. A bugle signaled, and the riders halted instantly. After a dramatic pause, four of the greatest chiefs, in spectacular war gear, rode through the lane. They saluted the commissioners with fists held high.

The flashing color of the feathered warbonnets and battle streamers and the thundering sound of the flying ponies stunned the commissioners. Never had they seen such horsemanship. Newspaper reporters later called it the greatest cavalry display ever witnessed.

The Comanche, the Kiowa, the Cheyenne, the Arapaho, and the Kiowa-Apache were all represented. More than eight hundred lodges filled the meeting ground when all the Indians had arrived. Only the Quohada Comanche had refused the invitation.

The council continued for two weeks. The Peace Commissioners wanted to stop the frontier wars and prevent the Indians from interfering with the construction of railroads across the plains. They asked the Indians to abandon their nomadic life and take up farming on reservations.

The idea was neither new nor popular with the tribes. Each day the generals met with the leading chiefs. They gave gifts and explained why this was the only way peace could be achieved. In the end, most chiefs signed the treaty. Quanah was among those who did not.

The Cheyenne and Arapaho were offered land south of the North Canadian River to the banks of the Washita. The Kiowa and Comanche were given three million acres between the Washita and Red Rivers. Ten Comanche chiefs put their marks on the white man's paper.

Quanah met many friends at the great council. He saw the gifts the generals gave to convince the chiefs to move onto reservations. He especially liked the tall, black stovepipe hat the general with the eagles on his collar gave Kicking Bird, chief of the Kiowa.

He listened to the eloquent words of Ten Bears, chief of the Yampareka:

"My heart is filled with joy when I see you here, as the brooks fill with water when the snows melt in the spring," he said to the generals. "I feel glad, as the ponies do when the fresh grass starts in the beginning of the year. . . . My face shines with joy when I look upon you."

After this flowery beginning, he got down to cases.

"It was you who sent out the first soldier, and it was we who sent out the second. Two years ago, I came upon this road, following the buffalo, that my wives and children might have their cheeks plump and their bodies warm. But soldiers fired on us, and since that time there has been a noise like that of a thunderstorm, and we have not known which way to go.

"So it was on the Canadian. The blue-dressed soldiers and the Utes came from out of the night, when it was dark and still, and for campfires they lit our lodges. Instead of hunting game, they killed my braves. . . .

"So it was in Texas. They made sorrow come into our camps, and we went out like buffalo bulls when the cows are attacked. When we found them, we killed them, and their scalps hang in our lodges. . . .

"The Comanches are not weak and blind, like the pups of a dog when seven sleeps old. They are strong and farsighted. . . .

"You said you wanted to put us on a reservation, to build us houses and make us medicine lodges. I do not want them.

"I was born on the prairie, where the wind blew free and there was nothing to break the light of the sun. I was born where there were no enclosures and where everything drew a free breath. I want to die there, and not within walls. I know every stream and every wood between the Rio Grande and the Arkansas. I have hunted and lived over the country. I have lived like my fathers, and like them, I lived happily.

"When I was in Washington, the Great Father told me that all the Comanche land was ours, and that no one should hinder us in living upon it. So why do you ask us to leave the rivers and the sun and the wind, and live in a house?

"Do not ask us to give up the buffalo for the sheep. . . .

"The Texans have taken away the places where the grass grew the thickest and the timber was the best. Had we kept that, we might have done the thing you ask. But it is too late. The white man has the country we loved, and we wish only to wander on the prairie until we die. . . ."

The generals were unmoved by Ten Bears' eloquence. Other great chiefs made similar speeches.

In reply, a white general told the chiefs, "The time has come for you to live in peace or face destruction by white armies."

The senator gave the government's promises. The Indians would receive reservation land, schools, farm equipment, cattle, and supplies for a period of thirty years.

He finished by saying, "You say you wish to do as your fathers did. You say that the buffalo will not last forever. They are now becoming few, and you must know it. When the day comes, the Indian must change the road his father trod, or he must suffer and die.

"We now offer you the way. Before all the good

lands are taken up by the whites, we wish to set a part of them for your exclusive use. On that land, we will build you a house to hold the goods we will send you when you become hungry and naked. You can go there and be fed and clothed."

Then the chiefs were invited to put their marks on the treaty paper. Those who signed did so not because they agreed with what the treaty proposed, but because they saw the free life on the plains coming to an end.

After his speech, Ten Bears came to Quanah. He was sad of heart.

"Quanah, there is no place for us now. We cannot live as we have in the past. Make your mark for the Quohadas."

Quanah's eyes flashed. "The land they give us does not include the great Staked Plains," he said. "That is where I live."

He scowled. "The Quohadas are free, Ten Bears. Tell the white chiefs that the Quohadas are warriors. We will surrender when the bluecoats come and whip us on the great plains. Not before."

Chapter

10

*Quanah Elected War Chief
of the Quohadas—1871*

The Medicine Lodge Treaty solved nothing.

Some tribes went to the reservations but could not adjust to the new life. Indian agents soon discovered that Indians would not eat butchered beef. The agents had to turn the cattle loose on the prairie so the warriors could hunt them as they once hunted buffalo, and the women could prepare the meat in the old manner.

The Indians accepted government rations during the winter months, but when the grass turned green in the spring, they rode away to follow the buffalo— and to raid for horses. Indian agents and soldiers constantly faced the problem of disciplining the tribes.

Chief Mow-way of the Buffalo Eaters told the agent at Fort Sill, "There's no reason for a Comanche to come back to the reservation until Comanches on reservations live better than Comanches on the prairie."

The Quohadas, still free on the Staked Plains, continued to raid. The Comancheros now paid a good price for beef as well as horses. The frontier was more turbulent than it had been before Medicine Lodge.

Quanah now entered the legends of Texas and the frontier as a notorious raider. He traded horses and cattle with the Comancheros for Winchester ten-shot repeating rifles, and soon his Quohadas were better armed than the cavalry. Ammunition, though, was expensive. The Comancheros demanded many head of cattle for each box. This forced more cattle raids.

As the Austin newspaper reported in 1870: "Farmers are shot down in their fields and their stock is stolen before their eyes. Not for twenty years have the Indians been so bold. . . . The frontier is breaking."

The troubles peaked in 1871. Anger ran like a disease throughout the tribes—those on the reservation and those who had stayed out. In early May, White Bear, Sky Walker, and other chiefs held a big meeting to talk about what had happened since the Medicine Lodge Treaty.

"More white men than ever cross our lands," White Bear said.

Sky Walker and White Bear called for a war party to drive the white men from their lands for all time. A hundred warriors joined them. The party set up a watch along the Butterfield Trail. That night, Sky Walker had a vision.

"Two groups of white men will come," he told the war party the next day. "We must not touch the first group, but we should destroy the second."

As in his vision, two parties of travelers came along

the trail that day. The first was a wagon escorted by a small cavalry detachment. General William Sherman was in the wagon, on his way to plan Army action against the Indians. Sky Walker held the warriors back, and the wagon passed unmolested. Sherman found out later that he owed his life to Sky Walker's dream.

The war party attacked the second group, a supply train of ten wagons. The teamsters tried vainly to put their wagons in a circle, but the Comanches struck too fast. Five wounded men escaped into the brush, but seven were killed, scalped, and mutilated. The Wagon Train Massacre rekindled the fury of the frontier settlers.

In 1869, with flames searing the frontier, President Grant had looked for an experienced, resourceful cavalry officer to lead the Army against the Indians. He found Colonel Ranald S. Mackenzie, a Civil War veteran just thirty years old, and ordered him to form a new regiment, made up mostly of black ex-slaves from the plantations of the South.

Within a year, Mackenzie turned these field hands into the Fourth Cavalry, the best black regiment in the Army. The Indians called them "buffalo soldiers" and called Mackenzie "Bad Hand" because he lost two fingers of his right hand in the siege of Petersburg during the war.

Now, in the late spring of 1871, Grant ordered Mackenzie to take the Fourth Cavalry to Fort Richardson to put a final stop to the Indian attacks.

A short time later, General Sherman went to meet

Mackenzie at Fort Richardson. Along the road, ghostly chimneys standing over charred cabins like tombstones reminded him of the devastation of the Indian attacks.

On the evening of his arrival at Fort Richardson, a wounded teamster staggered into the fort with the grisly story of the Wagon Train Massacre. The general felt his scalp tingle, knowing his party had passed the spot of the massacre only two hours before it happened.

Sherman was determined to suppress the Indians at any cost.

That summer, cattle and horses were scarce in the lands bordering the Staked Plains, forcing the Quohadas to search for better spoils. Bear's Ear, now the war chief of the Quohadas, led the clan away from their home territory, back to the area near Fort Richardson. In a series of quick raids, one only three miles from the fort, the Quohadas gathered a large herd of horses.

Word of the raids reached Fort Richardson, and a troop of cavalry galloped out of the fort at once in pursuit of the Indians.

They overtook the Quohadas near the Red River and attacked immediately. Bear's Ear went down in the first volley.

Quanah, riding with Bear's Ear, took command. "Take the horses to the river," he ordered.

Quanah and a few warriors fought off the troops until the horses were across the river. In the hot running battle, a bullet grazed Quanah's thigh, nearly knocking him from his horse, but he continued to fight.

When the stolen herd was across the river, Quanah raced after it. The troopers pulled up at the river and watched them go.

In camp that night, the Quohadas mourned the loss of Bear's Ear and celebrated their victory over the cavalry. They solemnly elected Quanah the war chief of the Quohadas.

Chapter 11

Colonel Mackenzie—
Indian Fighter—1871

By late summer of 1871, Mackenzie had turned the rough, black "buffalo soldiers" into a tough professional Indian fighting cavalry. On the night of August 2, under a bright moon, the Fourth Cavalry rode out of Fort Richardson in search of the raiding tribes and especially the greatest of the raiders, Quanah Parker.

The cavalry discovered that the Indians had spared little along the frontier. Dozens of new graves and charred ranches lined the trails, but the troopers found no fresh Indian signs. The Comanches had retreated into the Staked Plains once again. After six weeks, Mackenzie gave up and returned to Camp Richardson.

He now knew that to find the Comanches, the Fourth would have to ride into the Staked Plains, where no soldier had dared go before. As long as the Indian

raiders could disappear into the safety of the grass-
lands, they would never be defeated.

On September 25, eight companies of the Fourth
Cavalry, two of the Eleventh Infantry, twenty Tonkawa scouts, and a hundred pack mules gathered at
the Clear Fork of the Brazos River. The rumor that
they were headed for the dreaded plains made even
the toughest soldiers nervous.

The night before the troopers were to move out, a
daring Comanche raiding party hit the Murphy ranch,
twenty miles from the camp, taking a hundred and
twenty cattle and thirteen horses from under the noses
of Mackenzie's six hundred troopers. The ranchers
were loud in their disgust with the Army.

Mackenzie was furious.

The next morning the troopers headed directly into
Comanche territory. A day later they spotted a herd
of buffalo moving across the plain, and Mackenzie
knew that Indians must be close. That night the troopers slept with their guns under their blankets, loaded
and ready to fire.

Around midnight the ominous sound of thundering
buffalo hooves roused the sleeping soldiers. Lieutenant Robert Carter, in charge of the night guard, peered
into the darkness at the shadowy outline of a wall of
buffalo charging straight for the camp.

Carter ordered his guards to grab their blankets.
"Wave them like you're bullfighters!" he yelled.

The troopers ran toward the advancing herd,
screaming, shooting into the air, and waving the blankets. The buffalo pounded toward them like snorting,

unstoppable locomotives. When they were nearly on top of the terrified men, the leading buffalo veered away. For an hour, a river of bellowing buffalo flowed around both sides of the camp. The soldiers hunkered behind their wagons, watching fearfully until the last of the big animals galloped past.

Before turning in, Carter said to Mackenzie, "Buffalo don't stampede at night."

"Not unless they're driven," Mackenzie agreed. "But I didn't see any Indians behind the herd."

"No," Carter replied. "But I'm sure they were there."

The next day the Tonkawa scouts surprised four Quohada warriors watching the cavalry from nearby hills. The spies disappeared instantly, but now the troopers knew their every move was being watched.

The scouts were following a trail leading toward Canyon Blanco, a favorite Quohada campsite, when darkness forced them to make camp. They drove their wagons into a circle, with the mules in the center and the horses tethered at one side. The troopers slept near their horses.

Just as the moon disappeared, the night erupted in an earsplitting din. The troopers leaped from their blankets to see Quanah Parker leading his Comanches through the camp, shooting, yelling, and ringing cowbells. The Indians dragged large buffalo hides to scatter the campfires and overturn the wagons.

The groggy troopers fired at the shadowy figures, but missed the Indians in the darkness.

Quanah and half a dozen warriors rode straight to

the tethered Army horses. With one last fusillade of gunshots, they stampeded the animals and raced away in the dark.

At daybreak the troopers rounded up the horses that remained near the camp. By noon they knew that the Comanches had made a good haul. Seventy horses were missing—including Colonel Mackenzie's own fine gray pacer.

Furious at their losses, Mackenzie stormed, "He's making fools of us again."

Captain E. M. Heyl and Lieutenant Carter led a group to look for missing horses, and saw Indians driving a small herd in a canyon. The troopers rode in after them and found themselves surrounded by yelling Comanches. They had been lured into a trap.

The soldiers raced to a protected ravine, dismounted, and began to fire. When the Indians hesitated for a moment, Captain Heyl and seven troopers dashed for safety, leaving Carter and five men to fight alone. Forming a small circle, the six kept up a steady carbine fire. The Comanches held their distance but circled the troopers, cutting off any chance of escape.

"They were naked to the waist," Lieutenant Carter wrote later, "arrayed in all their war paint . . . with warbonnets of fur and feathers fantastically ornamented. Their ponies . . . were striped and decorated with gaudy strips of flannel and colored calico. Bells were jingling, feathers waving, and with jubilant, discordant yells that would have put to blush any Confederate brigade . . . they pressed on.

"Mingled with the shouts, whoops, and yells of the

warriors could be heard the strident screeching and high-keyed piercing screams of the squaws far in the rear of the moving circles."

Carter saw flashes of light coming from the Comanche band. He learned later that the flashes came from mirrors the chiefs held to signal the warriors when to advance or retreat.

The steady shooting held off the attackers, but Carter ordered his men to put their guns on rapid fire. The rapid-fire volley drove the Comanches back, so that the troopers could duck into an arroyo. Then the Indians attacked, with Quanah leading the charge.

"A large and powerfully built chief led the bunch," Carter wrote, "on a coal-black racing pony. Leaning forward on his mane, his heels nervously working in the animal's side, with six-shooter poised in air, he seemed the incarnation of savage, brutal joy. His face was smeared with war paint, which gave his features a satanic look. A large, cruel mouth added to his ferocious appearance.

"A full-length warbonnet of eagle's feathers spread out as he rode, descending from his forehead and back to his pony's tail, almost sweeping the ground. Large brass hoops were in his ears. He was naked to the waist, wearing simply leggings, moccasins, and a breechclout. A necklace of bear's claws hung about his neck. His scalp lock was carefully braided with otter fur and tied with bright red flannel.

"His horse's bridle was profusely ornamented with bits of silver, and red flannel was also braided in his mane and tail, but, being black, he was not painted.

Bells jingled as he rode at headlong speed, followed by the leading warriors, all eager to outstrip him in the race. It was Quanah, head war chief of the Quohadas."

Carter drew his Smith and Wesson revolver. "I fired several shots at a distance of not more than thirty feet, but the wily chief was on the other side of Private Gregg, guiding his pony by rapid zigzagging so as to make Gregg his shield. . . . I shouted at Gregg to pull his six-shooter, and he reached for it. But it was too late. A report from the chief's pistol now at Gregg's head—a fall—a thud—a tragic death."

Abruptly the Comanches whirled and raced for the mountains as Colonel Mackenzie and the rest of the Fourth charged up the canyon to Carter's rescue.

Carter received the Congressional Medal of Honor for fighting off Quanah's attack.

Late that afternoon the Tonkawa scouts found fresh tracks leading further up into Canyon Blanco. Mackenzie followed the tracks into the canyon the next morning and came to the hastily abandoned remains of the Quohada village.

After breaking camp the Quohadas had run up the canyon, crossing and recrossing their trail to confuse the Tonkawa scouts. The troops followed the confused tracks for several hours. The trails finally joined at one path that led to the rim of the canyon. The entire troop scrambled up the steep, slippery path to the rim, only to discover that the Comanches had taken another trail back down into the canyon. The troopers followed.

At the bottom the Comanches traveled a hundred

feet along the river, then climbed another steep path back to the rim.

"Those clever devils," Mackenzie growled as the troop climbed the canyon wall a second time. "They're killing our horses."

"They don't miss a trick," Carter said. "They know their light ponies can take it better than our big horses."

This time the trail cut out into the Staked Plains, making a wide bent-grass path. The scouts estimated that the Quohadas were driving two to three thousand horses. And in spite of the big herd, they moved fast, staying ahead of the troopers.

The Fourth followed them into the plain, a first for the cavalry. The troopers passed lodge poles, skins, stone hammers, and other baggage the Quohadas had discarded to lighten their loads. Occasionally Comanche warriors doubled back, riding parallel to the cavalry but out of range, ready to nip at anyone who fell behind. Mackenzie closed his columns.

Heavy clouds moved in and turned the day dark. The wind picked up, and a howling "blue norther" hurled rain, sleet, and snow at them. By the end of the day, five inches of snow covered the prairie. The weary horses slipped and staggered. Mackenzie finally ordered the group to pitch camp, in a defensive ring, as always.

The wind slashed and moaned through the darkness. Just as the weary, frozen troopers unrolled their blankets, a blast of gunfire broke out. From out of the storm, wildly whooping and hollering, Comanches swept up to the circle, taunting the soldiers and firing into the wagons. They disappeared like ghost riders into the whirling snow before the soldiers could take aim.

"They make me feel like an idiot!" Mackenzie raged, but there was nothing he could do.

By morning the weather was so bad that the colonel had to head back to Fort Richardson. His campaigning for the year was over.

The ride back was a bitter one. Quanah had taunted and outmaneuvered him, taken his horses, and still rode free on the Staked Plains.

In recapping the campaign, Mackenzie reported that his men had ridden 509 miles. They had done little damage, but for the first time, the Fourth Cavalry had penetrated the Staked Plains, the heart of Indian country. It was no longer feared, forbidden territory.

Chapter

12

Mackenzie Conquers the Llano Estacado—1872

Colonel Mackenzie's face was granite-hard as he listened to the frightened prisoner's story. Captured by a cavalry detachment during a fight with raiding Comanches, Polonis Ortiz spoke rapidly in broken English.

He said he was from New Mexico, one of fifteen Mexicans hired to steal Texas cattle. "We dress like Indians," he said. "Then people think these are Indian raids. There are many outlaw bands, white and Mexican, because the price of beef is high."

"You mean Indians aren't the only ones stealing cattle?" Mackenzie said.

"No, senor Colonel. We steal, then we trade with the Indians for cattle they steal. We drive cattle to New Mexico."

Mackenzie looked at a map on the wall. A large

blank space on the map was marked "Llano Estacado. Uncharted."

"How do Indians and outlaws get these cattle across the Staked Plains? There are no trails out there."

"Colonel, good road with plenty water crosses the plains. Only Indians know it. They take stolen cattle over it every day to Mexico."

"You know that road?"

"I ride many years on the plains," Ortiz said.

Mackenzie looked at him. "Ortiz, you can stay with me as my guide on the plains, or I can give you to the Texas Rangers. They'd be interested in outlaws who masquerade as Indians."

The color drained from Ortiz's face. "Not the Rangers, Colonel! I guide you. I know trails. I show you Indian camps. I show you where they drive horses and cattle."

Mackenzie passed Ortiz's information to Brigadier General C. C. Auger, now commanding the cavalry in Texas. "We're fighting more than Indians," he reported. "With renegade whites and Mexicans as well as Indians on the warpath, the number of cattle raids will grow."

Auger ordered Mackenzie to break up the outlaw bands and stop the Indian attacks. The colonel rejoined his troops, and the men of the Fourth, grim-faced, mounted up and headed out.

Mackenzie planned to go first into the Staked Plains after the Comanches, then hunt the outlaws in New Mexico.

◆　　◆　　◆

Quanah and his chiefs smoked the pipe in his lodge. Afterward, they listened to their scouts.

"Bad Hand and many buffalo soldiers ride into the Staked Plains from Fort Griffin," they said.

"They look for a big fight," Quanah said. "They think they can beat us that way."

"They have many guns that shoot without reloading," Buffalo Foot pointed out.

"We have guns like that," Mi-so told the chiefs. "It would be a fierce battle, but we would win. They don't know our lands. We would cut them down."

"Yes, Mi-so," Quanah said, "we could defeat them, but it would cost us many braves. We would both win and lose."

"Anyway, more bluecoats would come later," Buffalo Foot said. "We would have fewer warriors to fight them."

The chiefs thought about this as they passed the pipe around the circle again.

"It's not good to fight their way," Quanah said. "We'll fight our way." He proposed that they ride a day or two in front of the cavalry, leading them across the Llano Estacado but never allowing a pitched battle.

"We'll make them follow us," he said. "We'll wear them down the way the wind wears a hill of sand, a little at a time."

"But where will it end?" Mi-so wanted to know.

Quanah spread his hands flat. "We lead them to the mountains of the Apache in New Mexico. Then we go in small groups into the mountains where they can't track us."

The chiefs considered the plan and decided it was right.

The Fourth rode up onto the Staked Plains near Canyon Blanco in country they knew well, and kept going into land they had never seen before. The scouts continually found Indian signs a day or two old, and that made them wary. Strong scouting parties went ahead by day, and the troop camped with doubled guards at night. Tantalizingly, the Quohadas always stayed a day or two ahead.

The troopers crossed from Texas into New Mexico without finding the Quohadas. Past the western edge of the Staked Plains, the flat prairie turned into rolling hills. At Fort Sumner, on the banks of the Pecos, the troop took on supplies, then scouted farther west, to where the mountains rose up around old Santa Fe.

Before they reached the mountains, however, all signs of the Comanches disappeared. Day after day, the scouts came back with the same story. The Indians had simply evaporated. One day there would be tracks of a large band of Comanches; the next day, the tracks would be gone.

Mackenzie switched plans and began his search for the outlaws named by Ortiz. He found their camp abandoned.

As the troopers examined the empty campsite, John Hittson, a Texas cattle rancher, rode in at the head of ninety veteran well armed cowboys. They were driving a herd of 6,000 cattle.

"If you're lookin' for those thieves, you're a little

late," Hittson told the colonel. "We took care of them. Now we're taking our cattle back to Texas."

He added, "Seems you're always a little late, Colonel."

Mackenzie winced.

That night he summoned Ortiz. "We'll go back to Texas on your cattle trail. I want to know that road."

This was on August 19, 1872. By the 31st, after an easy trip, the Fourth camped at the mouth of Canyon Blanco, now a familiar spot. The trail had been as good as Ortiz promised, with plenty of nearby water.

The Fourth had now crossed the dreaded Llano Estacado twice by different routes, riding through country never before penetrated by soldiers. While Mackenzie had not found the Quohadas, he now had valuable maps that solved the mysteries of the great Staked Plains forever.

The Texans weren't impressed by Mackenzie's maps. They only knew that he hadn't killed any Indians. The *Gainesville Gazette* complained, "We had great faith that Colonel Mackenzie would teach the Indians a lesson they would not soon forget . . . and have anxiously waited to hear a good report from his command . . . but in vain. The Indians are committing more depredations in Texas today than when General Auger issued his order."

The criticism hurt. Mackenzie rested the Fourth for a couple of weeks, then headed out once more.

Indian signs again were scarce. "They make raids,"

the colonel grumbled, "but when I try to find them, they're nowhere to be seen."

On the fifth day, near McClellan Creek, Captain Davis, scouting along the bank, found a large patch of wild grapes. He dismounted and noticed grapes scattered beneath the vines. Someone had picked grapes here only a short time before.

He called the Tonkawa scouts to the spot. They soon found mule tracks and followed them to the Red River. A village of nearly three hundred lodges nestled in the river valley. Women dried buffalo meat, and children played nearby. Braves snoozed in the sun.

The Tonks said these were the Buffalo Eaters under Chief Mow-way. Mackenzie ordered an immediate attack.

Brandishing sabers, the troopers drove into the valley and hit the village. A second unit circled to the back of the village and rounded up the Comanche horses.

The fight lasted only half an hour. A few warriors fired at the troopers from the high grass, while others got to their horses and rode out. They attacked the troopers twice, but each time were driven back. After the battle, the troopers tallied 262 lodges destroyed, 52 braves killed, and 130 women and 3,000 horses captured.

Moving a couple of miles from the Indian camp, the Fourth turned in for the night among the sand hills, after corralling the captured Indian horses in a nearby gully.

◆　　　◆　　　◆

The bleeding brave ran into the Quohada camp, shrieking, "Long Knives! Long Knives!"

Quanah ran to meet him.

"Long Knives attacked Mow-way's camp," the boy panted. He imitated the way they brandished their sabers. "They've killed many Buffalo Eaters!"

Quanah summoned the chiefs. The Quohadas had followed Mackenzie back from New Mexico, and were preparing for an autumn buffalo hunt with Mow-way's band. Their camp was only a few miles from that of the Buffalo Eaters.

"This killing must be avenged," Quanah said. "Bad Hand must know fear of us once more."

He told the chiefs what they must do.

After dark, yelling, shooting Quohadas surrounded the cavalry camp, riding in a wide circle. The troopers fired at them, but the Indians stayed just out of range. Mackenzie waited anxiously for a full attack, but it never came. After several hours the Comanches rode off.

The next morning, Tonkawa scouts, who had been guarding the herd of captured Indian ponies, walked sheepishly into camp. They led a single burro piled high with their saddles. They had been caught while Quanah's warriors were surrounding the camp. Other Comanches had run at the corral and retaken the captured horses—along with the horses of the Tonkawas and some cavalry mounts as well.

"Quanah again!" Mackenzie snapped.

The Colonel returned to Fort Richardson with his

prisoners. Texans rejoiced at the news of his victory. At last Mackenzie had beaten the Comanches! The Texans ignored the embarrassing fact that Quanah had recaptured the horses and ridden from the battle site unscathed. But Mackenzie seethed. He had lost another round in the seemingly endless chess game with Quanah Parker.

Chapter

13

Adobe Walls—1874

More than two hundred raids were reported along the frontier in 1873. Quanah and his Quohadas ran wild on the Staked Plains. Raiders struck along all the cattle trails from the big Texas ranches to Colorado and Kansas. The fires of the Indian War blazed.

The Comanches ravaged south through Texas and down to Durango in Mexico in November. Returning the next month, they fought a bitter battle with a cavalry detachment in south Texas, losing nine braves and fifty horses. Continuing northward, they were challenged by another cavalry troop near Double Mountain. From this battle, only a handful of the raiding party rode home.

The Quohadas mourned their losses. It now seemed that wherever a raiding party went, the cavalry was waiting.

By spring The People were desperate. They were hemmed in by the cavalry, and they feared starvation as the big buffalo herds dwindled. Professional buffalo hunters killed the shaggy animals by the thousands, shipping railroad cars of hides east each week from railheads in Kansas. The stink of the rotting carcasses poisoned the sweet prairie air.

In the midst of this gloom, Esa-tai, a young medicine man, told the Quohadas of a vision. They should hold a sun dance, as the Kiowas and the Cheyenne did, which would give them great power to conquer the whites.

Quanah did not believe in the power of a sun dance, but he saw that it might unite the downcast tribes for a final drive against the intruders. The People, he knew, needed inspiration.

Mighty medicine was made at the sun dance. Esa-tai performed magic. "I am Esa-tai," he told the warriors, "son of the wolf. I talked with the Great Spirit, and he said, 'I will make the people strong, and they shall drive the white man away.'" Throwing his head back, Esa-tai uttered the long, eerie howl of the wolf.

Quanah assured The People, "Esa-tai came to the Quohada and proved his medicine. He told us when storms would come and where the buffalo would be. He told us when the long-tailed star in the sky would go away. What he said was true."

The People celebrated Esa-tai's promises with a great feast. He had wiped the bitter taste of defeat from their mouths.

In council, they set as their first target the hunters

who killed the buffalo near the Adobe Walls stockade. Esa-tai promised that the warriors would have an easy victory over the buffalo hunters.

The assembled tribes elected Quanah as their war chief. Nearly a thousand Comanche, Cheyenne, and Kiowa warriors rode behind him to Adobe Walls. Esa-tai, his pony covered with magic paint to protect it from bullets, rode with them.

Inside the stockade at Adobe Walls were Rath's trading store, Hanrahan's saloon, a blacksmith's shop, and the store of Leonard and Meyers. The hunters sallied into the plains from here to shoot and skin the buffalo, then brought the hides back for shipment to Dodge City.

At dawn on June 27, Quanah led his thousand warriors against the trading post.

The first arrows killed two white traders and their dog. The scalps of all three became Comanche trophies.

The hunters, including Bat Masterson and Billy Dixon, dashed for the protection of the buildings and began shooting through gun openings and over the walls with their powerful Sharps buffalo guns.

The heavy buffalo guns proved deadly. Six warriors fell in the first charge. The buffalo hunters watched openmouthed as Quanah galloped headlong through the gunfire, swooped to scoop up the lifeless body of a brave, and then raced for safety.

The Indians regrouped and attacked again. The murderous Sharps took their toll once more. Quanah sent charge after charge against the stockade throughout the afternoon, but each attack was driven off by the hunters' accurate fire.

Near sundown a shot shattered the rock behind which Quanah lay shooting at the stockade. A fist-sized piece hit him in the shoulder, and for the rest of the night his arm was paralyzed.

On the second day the Indians vainly continued charging. They tried twice to break through the stockade wall but were driven off. The marksmen dropped any warrior who came into their sights.

Esa-tai watched the battle from a hill he believed to be out of rifle range.

"Where is your powerful medicine?" Quanah asked bitterly near the end of the second day. "Where is the easy victory?"

Esa-tai said, "Some warrior has bad medicine. It has killed my powers."

Quanah turned from him coldly. At that moment, a buffalo slug hit Esa-tai's horse in the forehead, and it crumpled to the ground. The chiefs looked at the magic paint on the dead horse and turned away in disgust.

On the third afternoon the chiefs held a council on the butte above the stockade. As they surveyed the field below, a puff of blue smoke blossomed in front of the saloon. Before the crack of the rifle reached them, Chief Tohahkah, who was riding beside Quanah, toppled from his pony.

The miraculous shot stunned the chiefs. The hunters' medicine was too strong. Full of bitterness, Quanah ordered the warriors to withdraw.

Billy Dixon fired the shot that killed Tohahkah; it had traveled an astounding 1,538 yards. Historians have called it the shot that ended the Indian Wars. Many tribes, convinced they could not overcome medicine as powerful as this, turned to the reservation.

But Quanah led his people back to the fastness of the Staked Plains. They would continue to fight.

The battle at Adobe Walls stirred the wrath of Generals Sherman and Sheridan. They ordered Mackenzie to bring Quanah and his people to the reservation at any cost.

Now the most experienced Indian fighter on the frontier, Mackenzie drew his plan—he would squeeze Quanah from his lair. He sent Colonel Price to the northwest corner of the Indian Territory, with orders to move down the Canadian. He ordered Colonel Davidson to ride west from Fort Sill. Colonel Buell marched up the Red River. Mackenzie himself set out from Fort Clark.

This four-pronged attack would catch the Quohadas at some point, no matter where they were. The territory along the frontier and in the Staked Plains was covered. The end was only a matter of time.

Chapter

14

*The Tragedy at Palo
Duro Canyon—1874*

By September, 1874, the converging columns of cavalry had forced the Indians to retreat along the Red River, near the eastern edge of the Staked Plains. The Comanche were hard-pressed, fighting, and on the run.

As the pressure grew, many tribes gave up and went to the reservation. Quanah and his Quohadas defiantly stayed out. Mackenzie was determined to force him in.

On September 23, the Fourth climbed to the Staked Plains at the Caprock and headed out. Twice during the next few days, Comanches attacked at night in attempts to stampede the cavalry horses, but each time, the troopers drove them off.

During one attack, a Comanchero, José Tafoya, who was riding with the Comanches, was captured.

Mackenzie, who needed to know where the Comanches would camp for the winter, questioned him. When the Comanchero refused to talk, the buffalo soldiers hung him on an upright wagon tongue. Within moments, Tafoya agreed to tell the colonel how to get to the long-hidden Palo Duro Canyon.

Late on November 27, Mackenzie led his troops along a trail above Tule Canyon, knowing the Comanches were watching. After dark he abruptly changed course and headed for Palo Duro Canyon, following Tafoya's instructions. This was to be next to the last move in his deadly game with Quanah.

The troops rode all night and, at dawn, crept on hands and knees to peer for the first time down into the beautiful, secret Palo Duro. The sun turned the colorful walls into murals. At the bottom, along the clear stream, stood two hundred lodges. Secure in their canyon, the Comanches slept.

Mackenzie immediately saw why the Indians felt safe. Only one steep, narrow trail, a thousand feet long, led into the canyon. As they went down, troopers would be perfect targets for gunfire from the Indians below. Mackenzie hesitated a moment to calculate the odds, then ordered the first troops to start down. The troopers had to dismount and lead their horses down the steep path.

Three companies reached the canyon bottom before a sentinel fired a warning shot. One company reached the Indian grazing ground and cut the horses loose. Instantly the camp came alive with Indians—not only Quohadas, but Kiowas, Arapahos, and other Comanche bands who had fled from the troopers.

The warriors fought like tigers from behind rocks,

113

while the women escaped any way they could—through the canyon or up steep trails to the rim. The canyon became a junkyard, strewn with abandoned blankets, cooking utensils, buffalo robes, weapons, and clothing. Nearly two thousand horses, terrified by the din of battle, galloped wildly back and forth, trying to find a way out.

With Indians shooting from all directions and the only escape the steep path up to the rim, a frightened trooper hollered, "How will we ever get out of here?"

"I brought you in," the colonel replied, "and I will take you out."

The battle moved up the canyon. One after another, the warriors withdrew and scaled the canyon wall. By noon the troopers stopped the chase. They found the bodies of only four warriors. The rest had scrambled to safety.

The troopers now destroyed the lodges and everything in them. Smoky bonfires blazed up and down the canyon as buffalo hides, dried meat—everything the Comanches owned—was reduced to ashes.

Mackenzie looked at the herd of captured Indian horses and remembered Quanah's tricks. He knew the chief would come back to retake the horses. Mackenzie had been stung too often by this trick, and he now made sure it wouldn't happen again. He gave a few of the best to his scouts, then ordered the rest of the horses destroyed.

Firing squads were selected to do the job—cavalry troopers, men who loved horses and thought of them as companions. Tears streamed down their faces as they went about their deadly work. By the end of the day they had shot more than a thousand animals.

For fifty years afterward, a gruesome pile of horse bones marked the site of the Battle of Palo Duro Canyon.

Quanah and the Quohadas took paths they alone knew to get out of the Palo Duro. Once at the top, they fled deeper into the Staked Plains. They had no horses and no lodges. The buffalo meat they had stored for winter was destroyed.

Winter came early to the Staked Plains. One of the most brutal in Texas history, it hit The People at their most difficult moment. The bluecoats crisscrossed the trails of the Llano Estacado most of the winter, driving the Indians into hiding every time they attempted to move.

Slowly, stealing or capturing a horse at a time, they gathered a new herd. To survive, they scratched for food and hunted small game, deer, and antelope. By midwinter they had worked their way south to the warm climate of Mexico.

Quanah watched his people suffer, but his inner strength heartened the other Quohadas. Even when starvation was near, the band stood strong and refused to give up. In Mexico life was easier, and they became more determined than ever to stay clear of the reservation.

The Quohadas raided Mexican ranches and in a few months had a new herd of nearly 1,500 horses. For the coming summer, Quanah planned to take the Quohadas back to the Llano Estacado where they would live as they had always lived. They would go again to the beautiful Palo Duro and hunt freely across the plains. His heart hungered for a return to the old ways.

Quanah was very pleased by the new herd. The people were no longer thin and hungry. The terrible winter was passing from their memory. They could look forward to a good summer and the buffalo.

In April, High Buffalo and some Noconi warriors came from the north and feasted with them. The news they brought was bad. The Kiowas had gone to the reservation in February. Mow-way had taken his Buffalo Eaters in. In fact, all the tribes had made the trip to Fort Sill. Only the Quohadas and a few scattered individuals were still out.

Bad Hand and his bluecoats patrolled the Llano Estacado. There was no place on it they did not go. The colonel had sent a message from his fort to the Indians still out. If they came in immediately, they would not be punished. If they did not come in, he would exterminate them. There would be no mercy.

"Bad Hand speaks big words," Quanah said. "But he has never caught me."

High Buffalo shook his head. "Things are different now, Quanah," he said. "Even for me. I'm going from here to Fort Sill."

After High Buffalo left, Quanah looked at his people and saw the misery along with the pride in their eyes. The future was so uncertain. They looked to him for a decision. What should they do? It seemed they could never return safely to their beloved Llano Estacado.

Torn, Quanah went alone to a knoll away from the camp. He chanted, prayed, and called on the Great Spirit and on his medicine. He was the chief of The People. He wanted only freedom to live the old life, but plainly, the old life was gone and would never be again.

Should he continue to fight for it? If he did, he would lead his people to a certain death on the prairie.

Should he take them to the reservation? The thought of fences and digging in the ground sickened him.

His desire for freedom and his responsibility to The People wrestled within him like two battling warriors.

He prayed for hours, waiting for his answer.

Finally he looked up and saw an eagle overhead. It flew in sweeping circles. Quanah watched it with bated breath. After hovering uncertainly, the eagle suddenly plunged toward the earth. It disappeared behind distant trees, then suddenly shot skyward again. Even at this distance Quanah could see a snake clutched in its claws.

The snake, the ancient symbol of the Quohada! And the eagle, the sign of Quanah's medicine!

The great bird circled one more time, then wheeled to the east and flew from sight.

Quanah rose, gathered his pipe and medicine bag, and strode back to the camp. His heart was heavy, but he knew what he must do. The reservation lay to the east.

Chapter
15

*Quanah Leads His
People In—1875*

On June 2, 1875, a beautiful summer morning, Quanah rode to Fort Sill at the head of 407 Quohada Comanche warriors. Behind them were 1,500 horses, the wealth of The People. The families remained in the Staked Plains for now; Quanah would summon them when the time was right.

Colonel Ranald S. Mackenzie and his staff officers waited at the entrance to the fort. For Mackenzie, this was the final move in the match with Quanah.

The word that Quanah was coming in spread through the reservation like flames across the dry prairie. Hundreds of reservation Indians gathered to watch. They all understood the significance of this day. Quanah was the last of the great chiefs to come in.

When the Quohadas appeared, the Indian audience

cheered. Quanah waved to the assemblage, then rode straight to Mackenzie.

With quiet dignity, he said, "I have brought my people in. We will take up the white man's way."

With equal dignity, Mackenzie said, "We are glad to see you."

The two faced each other for a moment. Each recognized a worthy adversary in the other. Then Quanah turned and rode through the gate.

For 150 years, the Comanches had been the Lords of the Llano Estacado. Quanah had been perhaps the greatest of their leaders. Now Mackenzie watched with mingled feelings as Quanah rode into the fort. He had won a victory, but had not vanquished Quanah Parker. It seemed to him that they had only turned a page in the history books.

Later, looking back on his surrender, Quanah said proudly, "I came to Fort Sill myself. No one led me in like a cow. I fought Mackenzie. He was a brave man, a good soldier. But he had two thousand men. Me, I had only four hundred and fifty braves."

Chapter
16

Quanah Leads His
People Again—1876

The Comanche reservation at the edge of Fort Sill was a rectangle of wide, rolling plains, rich with grass and water. The purple-hazed Wichita Mountains stood behind it as a colorful backdrop. This land had been dear to the Comanches for centuries.

Even in this beautiful ancestral land, Quanah was sad and bitter at first. His people were full of discontent. His warriors, hunters for centuries, drew government rations every two weeks and could only dream of the days when they rode after buffalo across the plains.

They could not hunt, seek coups to build their fame, or tell of their deeds around the campfire. For them, there was no future. They lived, and yet they were dead.

No Comanche had ever planted a seed, and they

could not bring themselves to do it now. They hated the cornmeal issued to them and fed it to their ponies. They were given beef, but preferred buffalo meat.

Not understanding their inner suffering, still the government tried to help. In 1876, the Indian Agent gave sheep to The People. The Indians had no taste for sheepherding and didn't like lamb chops or mutton.

Comanche lodges, once made of buffalo skins, now were of government-issue canvas. Colonel Mackenzie built houses for the leading chiefs, but they would not live in them. Accustomed to life in the prairie, they camped in the yards and let their dogs sleep inside. Quanah, just in from the plains, was not offered a house.

The Indian Agent tried simulated hunts. Each brave chose a steer in a corral, and the steer was turned out. Riding as his father once rode after buffalo, the brave shot the steer from his running horse. The women butchered the steer where it fell. It was an unsatisfying substitute for a real hunt.

Chief Mow-way said, "We are soaring eagles learning to live like barn owls."

Dreams about his mother filled Quanah's sleep after he came to the reservation. Repeated dreams were messages to the Comanches. Quanah believed his medicine was telling him to visit his mother's grave.

Mr. Haworth, the Indian Agent, wrote a note for him to carry on his journey. It said, "This is the son of Cynthia Ann Parker. He is going to visit his mother's people. Please show him the road and help him as you can."

Quanah had been in the white man's world before only as a raider. Now he saw wondrous things: iron horses that pulled many people in houses on wheels; houses with houses on top of them; roads that crossed rivers. He was surprised that a white man's house was divided into many smaller houses inside.

White people stared at his Comanche features and were frightened. The Indian Wars were still fresh in their memories. But when he showed them his letter, he was treated more kindly. All Texans knew the story of Cynthia Ann Parker.

Silas Parker, Cynthia Ann's younger brother, welcomed him. Quanah lived with the Parkers through the summer, learning English and the white people's ways. He stayed in Cynthia Ann's room, slept in her bed, and often dreamed of her. He prayed by her grave.

At the end of summer, Quanah went to Mexico to visit his Uncle John, who had been captured at Fort Parker at the same time as Cynthia Ann, but by a different tribe. Years later he caught smallpox. The tribe, frightened by the disease, abandoned him. A Mexican slave girl stayed with him, and when he recovered, they married and went to Mexico, where he became a prosperous cattle rancher.

Uncle John welcomed Quanah warmly, and proudly showed him how they bred and raised cattle. Quanah liked the life on the ranch.

One afternoon as he crossed a corral, an angry Spanish bull charged him. The sight of the bellowing animal brought back old hunt memories, but Quanah was now on foot and unprepared. He dodged and ran for the fence. The bull caught him and threw him against a post. Ranch hands drove the bull away in time to save Quanah's life, but he received a nasty gash in his thigh.

Watching Uncle John's wife dress the wound, he said, "Worse than any hurt I got in battle. Bull worse than bluecoats."

As the autumn waned, he prepared to return to the reservation. John held a farewell fiesta that lasted two days, and gave him a horse with a fine Mexican saddle decorated in silver.

The trip north conjured up old memories, for he rode the old Comanche route across the Llano Estacado. Bitter north winds were blowing by the time he reached the agency.

He was full of stories about the good life he had seen.

Another chief, tiring of his stories, sneered and said, "If it was so good, why didn't you stay there?"

Quanah replied, "Down there I was just a plain Indian. Here I'm a great chief."

On his return Quanah received his beef ration—six live cows. He bought a branding iron like the ones he saw on Uncle John's ranch—his brand was a Q—and drove his new cattle to a valley near the camp. This was the beginning of his herd, which grew large through the years.

The young braves, hating reservation life, became rebellious. A group under a young warrior, Black Horse, left the reservation to raid in the summer of 1877. The cavalry rode out after them, cornering them near Casa Amarilla.

Quanah told Mr. Haworth, "Those young warriors will die fighting. If others admire what they do, we will go back to the old ways. Let me go talk to them."

Haworth agreed, and Quanah rode to Casa Amarilla. Dressed in his bison headdress and full war regalia, he rode into the battlefield. The braves allowed him to come to their lines.

Quanah smoked a pipe with them.

"We will die," Black Horse told him, "but we die as warriors. Better that than what happens to us on the reservation."

Quanah said, "If you fight now, you hurt all The People. We must learn the new ways. If we do not, The People will suffer and die in bad ways. If you come back with me, the others will try to learn the new ways."

Black Horse and the others argued a long time, but finally, with Quanah at their head, they rode past the assembled troopers and back to the reservation.

Mow-way was the head Comanche chief on the reservation. In 1878, he said to Quanah, "I am old. It is time for another to lead The People. The chiefs have chosen you, even though you are still a young man. Your white blood will be a bridge for us."

Horse thieves began to raid the Indian herds near Fort Sill. Since the Indians were not permitted off the reservation, thieves had only to drive the horses past the reservation boundary to be safe.

Quanah discussed the problem with Agent Haworth. "We have lost a hundred horses," he said. "I trailed a bunch to the Red River. I could have caught them."

The agent said, "Next time, cross the river and go after them."

"We are forbidden to go off the reservation."

"You must protect yourselves," the agent said. "Go take your horses back. If you catch the men, bring them to me and I will punish them."

Quanah felt good as he rode to his lodge. Now he could take action.

He and his friend, Sankadota, followed the trail of a stolen herd. The thieves had ridden fast until they crossed the reservation boundary, then they camped. At sundown Quanah and Sankadota caught sight of the herd.

In the old Comanche way, the two warriors crept up on the horses after dark. Then whooping wildly, they drove the herd through the camp to taunt the rustlers. Later the thieves discovered their own horses were missing along with the Indian ponies.

The word got around that the Indians could now take care of themselves. The pony raids declined.

School was a problem on the reservation. Comanches had always learned what they needed—to make arrows, to hunt, to read the wind—from their elders on the prairie. They saw no good in a school where teachers who knew none of these things taught the children from books.

Quanah had learned much visiting his uncles, and he knew that as he learned, his life became easier. He explained this to The People.

"Our children," he said, "will never hunt buffalo, so they do not need to learn how. But they must learn to talk to the white man and to do the things he does."

Around the fire one night, he and Sankadota smoked the pipe and talked about learning.

"I hear what you say," Sankadota said, "but the white man's school is foolish. They do not teach our boys to be warriors."

"Think of wild horses on the prairie, Sankadota," Quanah said. "When wild, they're no good for war. But after you train them, they fight well. School, I think, is the same."

Following Quanah's counsel, The People began to send their children to school.

Quanah had four wives when he came to the reservation, the number that tribal law said a chief could have. He built a lodge for himself, and near it, one for each wife. Handsome sons and daughters were born. When they were old enough, Quanah sent them to school—first on the reservation, and later to the famous Indian School in Carlisle, Pennsylvania.

Quanah told Agent Haworth he thought a real buffalo hunt might ease the misery of The People. Haworth gave permission for an autumn hunt. As the leaves turned crisp, the whole tribe set out for the old hunting grounds.

The hunters ranged across the prairie for weeks but found no buffalo. The few antelope and deer they killed were barely enough to feed them. When the snow began to fall, they still had not seen one buffalo.

Quanah led The People sadly and in silence back to the reservation. They knew now that the old life was gone. Without buffalo, they could never live on the prairie again.

Chapter
17

The Later Years—1885–1906

The Comanches owned thousands of acres of fine pasture land on the reservation, but since only a few raised cattle, much of it was unused. Now that the Indian threat was gone, Texas cattlemen expanded their herds and began to move them across the Red River to graze on the unused Comanche lands.

The Comanches became angry. It was the same old story. The white man moved in on Indian lands when he felt like it.

Quanah said, "When a white man takes something from another white man, he pays for it. Why not pay for grazing?"

The Agent liked the idea. He got the ranchers to pay the Comanches in live cattle for the grazing rights to their land. Each Comanche family was given a share of the animals received.

Quanah led the young warriors to the Red River to receive the first payment. They branded their cattle and took them back to the reservation.

Invited to eat with the cowboys at the chuck wagon, Quanah met Burk Burnett, the big cattle rancher. The two liked each other instantly and became lifelong friends.

Quanah visited the Burnett ranch often and met many white people. At first they were afraid or critical of him, but as they got to know him, their attitudes changed.

To Burnett, Quanah said, "White men need to meet Indians. Then they will like us better."

Burnett agreed and suggested that Quanah go to the annual Fat Stock Show in Fort Worth.

"You'll meet plenty of people there," he said.

Quanah wore his decorated buckskin tunic, leggings, and moccasins. Tonarcy, his wife, wove bright-colored feathers in his hair. He startled cowmen as he walked around Fort Worth. Most thought of the Indians as enemies, but here was one shaking hands and joking with them. Their fear disappeared, and Quanah knew at once that he was right.

He felt it was important for him to represent his people to the whites. He traveled often—to the Fat Stock Show every year, to Fourth of July parades in towns around Texas and Oklahoma, to any gatherings where people could see him and he could talk to them.

He led an Indian group to the New Orleans World's Fair. He traveled to Washington on Indian business.

His daughter and twenty young warriors went to the Chicago World's Fair.

"The more white people see us," Quanah explained, "the more they know we are not savages."

In Fort Worth, a man who had known the Parker family told Quanah that a picture of his mother had been taken.

A picture of his mother? Quanah had seen pictures but had never thought that there might be one of his mother. Now he wanted that picture very much.

Burk Burnett suggested that Quanah run an ad in the Fort Worth newspaper, asking anyone who knew of a picture of Cynthia Ann Parker to write to him.

Three weeks later the Agent received a package addressed to Quanah. It was from Captain Sul Ross, the Texas Ranger who had captured Naudah. The chief and the Agent opened the package together. Inside was Naudah's photograph.

Quanah gazed lovingly at the likeness. Though she wore a white woman's dress, and her hair was short, Naudah was still beautiful. She held little Tau-tai-yah in her arms. Her spirit touched Quanah.

A note in the package explained that this was a copy of a picture Ross owned.

Quanah asked the agent to write a note of thanks to Ross. "Tell him even though he took her away, my heart is glad toward him for this picture."

On a visit to Quanah's lodge, Burk Burnett said, "You ought to have a house, Quanah. Your children are learning the white man's ways. Living in a lodge is the old way."

Quanah agreed to consider the idea.

"Not only that, but you're the chief. The people would follow willingly if they saw you lived in a house."

"I could live in a house," Quanah said. "But I do not know how to build one."

Burnett said, "I'll take care of that."

A month later, wagons loaded with lumber came from Texas. Quanah picked a site at the foot of the Wichita Mountains and the men put up a square, two-story home. Airy verandas ran around three sides on both stories. The kitchen and dining room were in a separate wing on the fourth side.

The men painted the house white and the roof red. Quanah thought it needed something more and asked for a large white star on the roof of each wing.

The Indians had serious problems with the white man's courts. They didn't understand the laws or how justice was administered. They resented arrest by soldiers, often for breaking laws they knew nothing about. Courtrooms mystified them.

Quanah frequently had to explain the laws and the procedures to his people to soothe their smoldering resentment. Finally, in 1886, an Indian court was established.

Quanah was appointed a judge, along with Lone Wolf, a Kiowa chief, and Jim Tehuacana, a Wichita. The court dealt with smaller troubles. Murder and other serious cases were tried by the U.S. Commissioner at Wichita Falls.

Justice in the new court followed tribal customs. It was often more severe than white justice, but Indians liked being judged by their own people. Quanah sat as a judge until the court was disbanded in 1901.

Some Indians, like Quanah, had many wives. White law, however, said that no man should have more than one wife. The Commissioner of Indian Affairs ignored the problem for a long time, but finally felt he had to do something about it.

He decreed that any man with more than one wife must choose one and send the others back to their own families.

Quanah at this time had three wives.

The Commissioner said, "I hear you haven't complied with the order on marriages. You must choose one wife and tell the others to go."

"Tell my wives to go away?" Quanah said in mock astonishment. "Are you serious about this?"

"You can have only one wife," the Commissioner repeated. "Tell the others to go away."

Quanah looked at the floor, apparently in deep thought. Then he looked up, grinning.

"You tell 'em."

Nothing was ever said to Quanah again about his wives. During his life, Quanah had seven wives and fifteen children. Two of his wives were with him when he died.

In the 1800s, land-hungry settlers demanded that the prairies be opened to homesteaders. A commission proposed to the Cheyenne and Arapaho that each tribe member receive his own 160 acres of land. The tribe would sell the rest to the government to open for settlement. The Indians agreed.

So on April 22, 1889, ten thousand people lined up at the edge of the Indian territory (now Oklahoma) to claim the land the government bought from the tribes. A cannon boomed and the settlers raced—on foot, on horses, on bicycles, any way they could—for the land. The first man to claim a piece of land got it, while the rest rushed to the next plot. The race kept up until all the land was taken. Those who got there first were called Sooners—because they got there sooner.

Next, greedy eyes turned to the Comanche land. Quanah opposed breaking up the reservation, because he believed it best for the tribe to continue to lease its land for grazing. He enlisted the aid of his cattle-ranching friends, who helped not only because he asked them, but also because they didn't want "nesters" carving the open range into little farms. They succeeded in stalling the issue for a while.

In 1897, the thirty-year guarantees of the Medicine Lodge Treaty came to an end. Quanah went to Washington, D.C., to ask President McKinley to renew them for five more years.

"My people are not yet ready to live as independent citizens," he said. "Maybe half are ready, but not all."

The President said, "You yourself have said that the Indians must learn to live with the white man. Now the time has come."

And he hurried from his office to another meeting.

Quanah fought his land battle for eight years, but on June 6, 1900, Congress passed the law that broke up the reservation and gave each Comanche his own 160 acres of land. Homesteaders drew lots for the rest of the reservation.

Quanah often took part in local affairs. In 1901, he became president of the Parker School Board and donated land for a school near his home. In 1902, he was elected deputy sheriff at Lawton, Oklahoma. As time went on, his herds grew and he became prosperous. His children were educated, and two of his daughters married wealthy cattlemen.

Quanah was invited to lead a band of Comanches in a big parade in Oklahoma City at the first reunion of the Rough Riders, the volunteer cavalry unit organized by Theodore Roosevelt during the Spanish-American War.

The chief rode in full war dress at the head of the Comanches. After the parade, a brilliant display of fireworks awed and delighted the Indians, who had never before seen fire trailing across the night sky.

Later, in the hotel, Quanah met Colonel Theodore Roosevelt, then governor of New York. The two became close friends.

Roosevelt became vice president under President McKinley. A great outdoorsman, the colonel loved to hunt, and whenever he could, he hunted with Quanah on the Comanche reservation. In the summer of 1901, he was with Quanah when the news flashed that President McKinley had been assassinated. Roosevelt was now president.

In 1904, Roosevelt ran for a second term. He campaigned across the country, making speeches from the observation platform of a special train. In Oklahoma, he spotted Quanah in the crowd and invited him to the platform, where he threw his arm around the chief's shoulder and introduced him.

Quanah patted him on the back and told the crowd, "He is some man. He's the big chief of all of us."

The following January, Quanah rode up Pennsylvania Avenue in Washington, D.C., in the parade that celebrated Roosevelt's inauguration.

In 1906, Quanah helped Burk Burnett buy railroad right-of-way from the Comanches for a railroad across their pasturelands. The Quanah, Acme, and Pacific Railway was completed in 1910. It ran from the town of Quanah, Texas, named for the chief, to Dallas. Quanah rode the first train to attend a huge celebration at the Dallas State Fair.

Quanah loved that railroad. He often referred to "my train" or "my engine" and owned stock in the company.

Chapter

18

The Last Years—1907–1911

In 1907, Quanah felt the end of his life approaching, and he recalled the ancient Comanche custom of sleeping three nights in one's birthplace before death. He made a pilgrimage to Laguna Sabinas, where he had been born.

Much had changed since his last visit. Ranches lined the road through what had been open prairie. Quanah now drove in a new car. The last time, he had ridden a war pony in a raiding party.

Quanah left his car, walked to the shore of the lake, and in a clearing took off his white man's clothes. He put on a breechclout and moccasins. Lighting his pipe, he sent puffs of smoke to the Great Spirit.

"O Great Spirit," he chanted, "I come to you now because my time is nearly done."

For three days Quanah thought of the days of his

life. He remembered his victories and his sad ride to the reservation when freedom ended. It came to him that he had filled a need. The Great Spirit had given him the task of leading his people into their new life. Now his mission was accomplished.

On the last day, he chanted, "O Great Spirit, my work is done. I am ready to come to you."

Then he drove back to the house with the white stars on the roof.

Quanah thought often of his mother in these late years and wanted her near him. He arranged to have her body and Tau-tai-yah's moved from Texas. Reburied near his home, Naudah was back with her people, as she had so often begged to be.

On the night of February 22, 1911, Quanah fell ill with pneumonia. The tribal medicine man did what he could, but through the evening hours, Quanah's strength failed.

He told his family, "I am ready." Then he died.

Three times during the night, Quanah's wife Ton-arcy prayed to the Great Spirit. At dawn she called the family together as the medicine man chanted the Comanche funeral dirges.

For burial, Quanah was clothed in his full Comanche war regalia. A procession of mourners over two miles long accompanied the casket to the little white Post Oak Mission Church, in the shadow of the Wichitas. He was buried beside his mother and his sister.

Quanah Parker was the last of the great Comanche

war chiefs. During his life he had built a bridge for his people between the red man's world and the white. After his death, the government established a tribal committee to handle the affairs of The People.

Quanah Parker was the last chief of the Comanches.

Historical Note

Hundreds of histories, eyewitness reports, and reminiscences have been written about the Comanches from 1850 through 1875. While they agree in general fact, they differ considerably in details.

One conflict concerns the death of Peta Nocona. A report by Captain Sul Ross after the Battle of Pease River indicates that he believed he had killed Peta Nocona during the battle. Other accounts show that Peta Nocona was hunting at the time of the battle and died a year later.

Another deals with Quanah Parker's life from the time he was orphaned until he emerged as a Quohada chief. There has been much speculation as to which bands he lived with and how he joined the Quohadas.

In any doubtful case, our story follows the facts as

presented by Zoe Tilghman in her book, *Quanah: The Eagle of the Comanches*, published in 1938. Mrs. Tilghman, a reliable reporter, knew Quanah Parker and spoke with him frequently. Her husband was the famous Marshal Bill Tilghman, a frontier lawman, who also knew Parker and lived for many years in the Comanche lands.

Glossary

Bridal price. It was customary for a young brave to offer a number of horses to the father of the girl he wanted to marry. If the father accepted the offer, the marriage was considered accomplished, and the brave took the girl to his lodge.

Comanche bands. The Comanche tribe was divided into a number of bands—such as the Quohadas, the Honey Eaters, and the Noconi. Each band was a separate unit with its own chiefs. There was no chief over the whole Comanche nation. Warriors were free to move from one band to another at any time.

Comancheros. Traders who came north from Mexico to trade with the Comanches (and other tribes) were called Comancheros. Because they accepted horses and cattle they knew were stolen, and provided the only active market for such goods, they were considered illegal traders by Texans and the U. S. government.

Coup. Pronounced "coo," the word came to the Indian language through early French-Canadian trappers, the *voyageurs*. To a Comanche, a coup was any especially good or brave feat. To *collect coups* would be to perform brave feats.

Llano Estacado. The great plains of grass that extended from the Red River, near the Oklahoma Border, south almost to the Mexican border—covering virtually all of western Texas—were called the Llano Estacado by early Spanish explorers. The name means the Staked Plains, so-called because the huge area was a sea of grass so vast that riders often lost their way. The padres accompanying the Spanish explorers marked trails across the plains by driving stakes into the ground. The Llano Estacado remained a mystery until Colonel Mackenzie mapped them for the first time during his pursuit of Quanah Parker.

Remuda. The word comes from the Spanish and means a herd of horses from which one is chosen for the day. A stagecoach remuda would be a herd of horses from which fresh ones were picked each day. The Comanche measured their wealth in horses, and each band turned its horses into a common pasture to graze. While each warrior had his favorite horse, new ones or replacements were often selected from the herd.

Slaves. The Comanches often took captives—men, women, or children. Some were eventually adopted into the tribe and became as Comanche as the Comanches themselves. Others were used as slaves to do heavy, menial work, were beaten and mistreated, and lived only a short time.

The People. The Comanches thought of themselves as "The People." The name Comanche was given to them by the Spanish early in the history of the West, but the tribes never accepted the name for themselves.

Travois. Pronounced "trav-wah," this was another word from the French-Canadian trappers. A travois was a vehicle for hauling heavy loads. It consisted of two long poles, one fastened to each side of a horse or mule. The back ends of the poles dragged on the ground. Household goods were placed on slings or in baskets suspended between the poles.

Bibliography

Bechdolt, Frederick E. *Tales of the Old-Timers*. New York: The Century Company, 1924.

Carter, Captain Robert G. *On the Border with Mackenzie*. Washington, D.C.: Eyenon Printing Company, 1935.

———. *The Tragedies of Canon Blanco*. Washington, D.C.: Gibson Bros., 1919 (personal reminiscence privately published).

DeShields, James T. *Cynthia Ann Parker: The Story of Her Capture*. St. Louis: "printed for the author," 1886.

———. *The Fall of Parker's Fort*. Waco, Texas: E. L. Connolly, 1972 (an extract from DeShields' *Border Wars of Texas*, published in 1912).

Dillon, Richard H. *North American Indian Wars*. New York: Facts on File, Inc., 1983.

Dobie, J. Frank. *The Mustangs*. Boston: Little Brown, 1952.

Edmunds, R. David. *American Indian Leaders*. Lincoln: University of Nebraska Press, 1980.

Fehrenbach, T. R. *Comanches: The Destruction of a People*. New York: Alfred A. Knopf, 1974.

Fletcher, George S. *How the Plains Indians Lived*. New York: David McKay Company, 1980.

Foreman, Paul. *Quanah, The Serpent Eagle*. Flagstaff, Arizona: Northland Press, 1983.

Gilles, Albert S., Sr. *Comanche Days*. Dallas: Southern Methodist University Press, 1974.

Gonzalez, Catherine Troxell. *Cynthia Parker, Indian Captive*. Austin, Texas: Eakin Press, 1980.

Hagen, William T. *Indian Police and Judges*. New Haven: Yale University Press, 1966.

——. *United States-Comanche Relations: The Reservation Years*. New Haven: Yale University Press, 1976.

Hill, Edward E. *The Office of Indian Affairs, 1824–1880: Historical Sketches*. New York: Clearwater Publishing Company, 1974.

Jackson, Clyde L., and Grace Jackson. *Quanah Parker: Last Chief of the Comanches*. New York: Exposition Press, 1963.

Jones, David E. *Sanapia: Comanche Medicine Woman*. New York: Holt, Rinehart & Winston, 1972.

Kelton, Elmer. *The Wolf and the Buffalo*. Garden City, New York: Doubleday & Co., 1980.

Leckie, William H. *The Buffalo Soldiers*. Norman: University of Oklahoma Press, 1967.

Lee, Nelson. *Three Years Among the Comanches*. Norman: University of Oklahoma Press, 1957.

Marriott, Alice, and Carol G. Rachlin. *Peyote*. New York: Thomas Y. Crowell, 1971.

May, Julian. *Quanah, Leader of the Comanche*. Mankato, Minnesota: Creative Educational Society, 1973.

Newcomb, W. W., Jr. *The Indians of Texas, from Prehistoric to Modern Times*. Austin: University of Texas Press, 1961.

Nye, Wilbur Sturtevant. *Bad Medicine and Good: Tales of the Kiowas*. Norman: University of Oklahoma Press, 1962.

———. *Carbine and Lance: The Story of Old Fort Sill*. Norman: University of Oklahoma Press, 1937.

———. *Plains Indian Raiders*. Norman: University of Oklahoma Press, 1968.

Rachlis, Eugene. *Indians of the Plains*. New York: American Heritage Publishing Company, 1960.

Richardson, Rupert N. *The Comanche Barrier to South Plains Settlement*. Glendale, California: Arthur H. Clark, 1933.

Sandoz, Mari. *The Buffalo Hunters*. New York: Hastings House, 1954.

Tilghman, Zoe A. *Quanah: The Eagle of the Comanches*. Oklahoma City: Harlow, 1938.

Wallace, Ernest. *Ranald S. Mackenzie on the Texas Frontier*. Lubbock: West Texas Museum Association, 1964.

Wallace, Ernest, and E. Adamson Hoebel. *The Comanches, Lords of the South Plains*. Norman: University of Oklahoma Press, 1952.

Webb, Walter Prescott, ed. *The Handbook of Texas*. Austin: Texas State Historical Association, 1952 (Quanah Parker entry: Volume 2).

Weems, John Edward. *Death Song: The Last of the Indian Wars*. Garden City, New York: Doubleday & Co., 1976.

White, Jon Manchip. *Everyday Life of the North American Indian*. New York: Holmes and Meier Publishers, 1979.

Wood, Norman B. *Lives of Famous Indian Chiefs*. Aurora, Illinois: American Indian Historical Publishing Co., 1906.

Wright, Muriel H. *A Guide to the Indian Tribes of Oklahoma*. Norman: University of Oklahoma Press, 1951.

```
        0
        1
    D   2
    E   3
    F   4
    G   5
    H   6
    I   7
    J   8
```